I0410181

Namibian Wildlife

An Alternative Guide for the Traveller on Safari

By

Sean Nicholson

www.mombolo.com

To Rose, Beth, Alec and Christopher with all my love and thanks for travelling with me.

Table of Contents

Introduction

A bit of scene setting first. Namibia is found in the bottom left hand corner of Africa (I know you know that but it had to be said). It is pretty big. It covers 823680 km2. Thanks to the Caprivi strip the country has a funny shape. One advantage of this is that the symbol for Namibia in the local sign language is a flat hand with fingers pointing down and thumb sticking out. North to south is around 1320 km. Two world famous deserts occupy much of the country - the Namib and the Kalahari. If the land is not desert, then it is arid scrub. An exception to this is the top right corner which has things like forests and swamps that do not exist elsewhere in the country.

Just to add emphasis to this issue of aridity you need to understand there are no perpetual rivers inside Namibia, but ironically some of the biggest rivers on the continent like the Zambezi, Okavango and Orange Rivers run along its borders. Within the country there are many riverbeds but these only have water once a year, once a decade or at even longer intervals. I do wonder if I am using the correct technical term here – surely sandbed or some other terms would be more accurate than riverbed.

This aridity has made Namibia popular with geologists. In most parts of the world geologists have to first battle with the large amounts of plant material and remove topsoil before even getting a sight of the rocks underneath. There is none of that in Namibia. Driving along you can see the various layers of rock building up in the hills and mountains either side of you. Given how easy it is to see the inside of the earth here you or I could innocently believe that we too could be a geologist in Namibia.

The Tropic of Capricorn passes just below the centre of the country. This along with the use of words like 'desert' and 'arid' leads everyone to believe the place is a fiery furnace. Indeed it can be with temperatures of 40 degrees celsius not being uncommon in the summer. This is just a cunning environmental trap for the unwary tourist. Popular destinations like Swakopmund are often covered in fog. This fog rolls in off the cold Benguela current and make jumpers, rather than sun glasses, the thing to pack. It gets colder. Try a night camping in the desert and you will need more than a jumper. Deserts get very hot by day but very cold by night. In the capital Windhoek you are 2000 metres above sea level. Here the kettle boils quicker, and making a cake rise is a greater challenge than at sea level. On the coldest winter days you need to scrape the ice off your car in the morning and light a log fire in the evening.

Namibia is not only big, but it is pretty empty. The population is just under two million people. Most of these live in the big towns or in the north of the country. That leaves very large areas with very few people. English is the official language but that has not been the case for many years and many people speak two or three of over a dozen local languages.

The country is stable, and democratic. In a world wide survey Namibia was rated 29th out of over 100 countries for being corruption free. This was ahead of some European countries and most of Africa, Asia and South America. There are good roads and other infrastructure. On the minus side, practically no one flies here directly. They normally come via South Africa.

Meat and alcohol are cheap, vegetables are expensive. The beef is the best I have ever tasted and I wish the bread could be as good.

Enough of the talking – if you want to learn more get a Namibian travel guide book. This book does not aim to cover the ground that others have covered better. Let's get on with the main course – the wildlife. You may want to read this keeping an african wildlife guide book handy (see Recommended Reading at the end). This will give you all the facts like height, weight, range, and appearance of the animal. None of that sort of stuff will appear in what follows. I am not a zoologist, instead I have stuck to the intrigue, rumor and gossip that I find fascinating about the animals in Namibia. So please enjoy.

Mammals

Cheetah

A bushman story says that one day God held a race between the tsessebe and the cheetah. Tsessebe (like other hartebeest family members) was very fast. Cheetah fearing for his soft paws borrowed some shoes from a wild dog. The race started and tsessebe easily took the lead, but just when it looked a certain result tsessebe fell. Being a generous fellow cheetah stopped to help tsessebe up. God was so impressed by this that he made cheetah the fastest animal, and let him keep the wild dog's paws. To this day cheetahs have claws just like dogs i.e. they cannot be retracted back into their paw like other cats, and of course they are still the fastest.

Cheetahs are big in Namibia. The biggest population in the world is here. Curiously they tend to be found on farms rather than in reserves. The centre of the country is their stronghold. All in all this makes cheetahs rather difficult to see. They live in public places like Etosha but at pretty low densities. The belief is that in Etosha they have to compete with bigger predators like lions and hyenas that steal the cheetah's kills, and also kill their cubs. Legend has it that the cheetah's tears (black lines running down from their eyes) are because they loose so many cubs. The larger predators like lions are not present on farms. The cheetah's prey like kudu and springbok are also relatively common on farms. So the cheetahs have a much better life on the farms than in the protected parks. The exception to this seems to have been the reserve round Hardap Dam in the south. The cheetahs here did so well that the game came under intense pressure from them and the cheetahs had to be removed. Of course there were no lions to compete with them at Hardap.

The cheetah has its own champion in the shape of the Cheetah Conservation Fund (CCF). These guys (should I say girls) have their headquarters about an hour east of Otjiwarongo in the shadow of the

Waterberg plateau. The centre attracts good funding from abroad, and it shows. They have an excellent museum-style exhibition about cheetahs and good research laboratories. They also have holding pens for cheetahs that are being relocated. Many farmers still perceive the cheetah as a threat to livestock so either kill them or want them removed. The CCF have done extensive research to help identify problems and solutions surrounding the issues of cheetahs living on farmland.

The research has produced some interesting discoveries and theories. Traditional dogs used with livestock flocks tend to be herders by instinct rather than guarders. When a predator like a cheetah appears herding dogs tends to group the livestock together and move them away. In effect they make the flock run away which triggers the predator's instinct to chase and kill. Guarding dogs have a different instinct. They approach the predator and bark. In this way the herd stays put rather than runs away. Cheetahs are not particularly brave, so they get scared off. This approach to protection may be more of a problem with leopards who enjoy eating dogs! The CCF now breeds big Anatolian shepherd dogs for Namibian farmers to use with their herds as guard dogs.

Over the years it has become clear that Namibian cheetahs have something called "playtrees". These playtrees are trees that cheetahs return to time and again. Often they have been used for many years and may be used by more than one group of cheetahs. Whilst cheetahs elsewhere in Africa use trees for climbing and playing, they do not use specific trees time and again like in Namibia. The Namibian cheetahs seem to have a strong urge to get to the playtrees and farmers use this to help trap them. They surround the playtree with a ring fence made of thorn bush branches, but leave a gap to get through. The gap contains a trap and when the cheetah goes through it is caught.

Namibian Cheetahs tend to be more social than those elsewhere. On average they are seen in groups of five but the record was a sighting of eighteen together.

Farmers are slowly learning to live with the cheetah and adapting some of their farming way to make room for coexistence. Ironically it is the game farmers with their big fences and valuable game (that the Cheetahs kill) which may produce a greater conflict with Cheetahs in the future.

Seeing a wild cheetah is difficult. You might at Etosha but you would have to be very lucky. Okonjima have radio collared cheetah they can track down for guests. Many of the lodges have captive cheetah that you can see being fed. At places like Dusternbrook and Harnas you can drive into the cheetah enclosure for good views as they are being fed.

Springhare

These cute animals are missed by many visitors because they only come out at night. They are widespread in the country where ever you get soil suitable for digging in. Go out for a walk with a torch at night, or drive around using your car headlights to find them. You are looking for a pair of small green luminous balls low down near the ground (their eyes). Springhares hop in a similar way to kangaroos. This means that you see bright green lights bouncing up and down in the dark - a wonderful and intriguing sight, especially if you do not know what is causing it.

A local sport for young Afrikaans males was to go out chasing springhares at night. You drive in your bakkie (four wheel drive truck) looking for the green eyes. Once found you jump out of the bakkie and run after the springhare trying to catch it before it gets to it's burrow entrance. Given the number of holes, big and small in the bush, this can be a risky business. Springhares are not quite the agile animals you would first suspect. They do not twist and maneuver that well which makes them a bit easier to catch. However they never venture far from their burrows.

Springhares dig burrows into the earth and seem to have two sorts of burrow. The normal type that slopes down and emergency escape ones that go vertically down. The thought that fascinates me is how does a small animal dig a vertical burrow? It would seem to be a rather tricky thing to do without getting stuck like some carrot with a hairy tail sticking out of the ground. Springhare have a clever trick of rapidly filling up a burrow entrance to deter would be predators from entering. As you can imagine, anything this cute has a lot of predators!

Countries like Kenya in East Africa are a long way from Namibia. To get to them you must cross the mighty jungles and rivers of central Africa. Surprisingly there are a number of mammal species that occur in both areas but no where else in Africa. The springhare is an example of one of these. Other examples include the aardwolf and the dik-dik. Not exactly animals which are big on long distance migration. What they have in common is that they are all species that prefer dry sandy soils. At some time long ago it is presumed that parts of Africa were drier and that the two regions were connected. Since that time life has got wetter and families have become separated.

A similar pattern is shown in other groups of animals. For example the kori bustard occurs in Southern and East Africa, but the two populations are separated by the vast woodlands in between.

Gemsbok

Namibia's national animal is a warrior of the vast deserts that occupy the country. They can be found amongst massive sand dunes and on the flat stony plains. They do not sweat, and only start panting when their body temperature goes over 40 degrees centigrade. Like mad dogs and Englishmen, gemsbok come out in the midday sun. Whilst they are plentiful in places like Etosha, you need to see them against the red Kalahari sands to truly appreciate their magnificence. I can truly understand their association with unicorns in this habitat.

The long horns can be very dangerous. Lions and people have been killed by them, and they can go through the sides of a modern car. By antelope standards gemsbok may even be considered aggressive. They are difficult to kill, even with a gun, and like some terminator can keep coming at you even after a couple of pistol shots have hit them! I am told the way to make sure they are dead before you get too close is to watch for their body hair going erect.

Rumour has it that baby gemsbok are born with horns - a painful birth if it were true. In fact the horns grow quickly and the babies hide for the first few weeks, so most people never see anything but youngsters with short horns.

Just to make life confusing gemsbok are also called oryx. You often hear children on game drives say "look an oryx", then another child will say "and there's a gemsbok as well".

Of great interest with any antelope are its toilet functions. When looking at antelope droppings you may also see a dark mark where the animal has urinated at the same time as defecating. This often gives a clue as to the sex of the animal. With females the urine will be close to the droppings, for males the urine will be a little way in front of the droppings. This reflects the different arrangements of body parts used for urinating and defecating. In dry places like deserts the urine can often cause the sand to stick together forming solid blocks in the shape of the urine puddle. The loose sand round these blocks can be blown away to reveal a sort of urine sculpture.

What is the "normal" population density for a species like the gemsbok that lives in such harsh environments? Questions like this matter for wildlife management and conservation but they are difficult to answer and seem to be dependent on factors beyond the control of those managing the animals. Some figures from the Namib Desert Park show the problem. At the end of the 1960's the park had an estimated 2000 game animals (mainly gemsbok, springbok, and mountain zebra). Then a series of good rainfall years from 1973 to 1978 swelled this population to an amazing 12000 animals i.e. a 600% increase. At the start of the 1980's the rains were very poor and the population collapsed down to around 1500 individuals.

Kudu

You can't help wondering if Namibia should have the kudu on its coat of arms rather than the gemsbok. This is only because of their high density and great attractiveness. In a way they seem more like a royal family to the warrior nature of the gemsbok. Going for a walk in the bush and coming across a male kudu 20 metres from you is a highly inspiring experience and gives a feeling of majesty that you don't get from a gemsbok. Just remember you can use up a whole roll of film on kudu, no problem.

The Namibian kudu is the greater kudu. There is a lesser kudu in case you were wondering, but not in Namibia. Kudu like scrubby bush, and hills are a bonus. The kudu population has increased massively since the 1950's. Their natural predators have decreased or disappeared and their competitors for browsing like rhino have also disappeared. Overgrazing by cattle has increased the scrubby nature of farmland again favoring the kudu, and farmers have built more waterholes once more helping the kudu. Whilst some of their cousins have problems with the fences put up by farmers, kudu just bound over them. One of the glorious sites when driving round the country is to see kudu effortlessly jumping these big fences with grace and ease. You can easily understand how they can jump into a windscreen, as regularly happens.

When I first arrived in Namibia I read an article explaining that kudus were not really that big a problem since only 4% of car crashes are due to kudus! 4% seemed pretty big too me. The kudu is the second biggest antelope in Africa. Kudu are pretty common, particularly on the roads south of Etosha down to the coast and across to Windhoek i.e. the main area for tourists. They like to graze at night beside the roads and when suddenly scared by a car will take flight in any direction, including towards the car. Now add the fact that kudus are magnificent jumpers and through either blind panic or supreme optimism will try and jump over your 120km/hr car. The end result is lots of accidents caused by kudus jumping on to car bonnets. The high jumping means not only do they land on your bonnet, but many of them go through the windscreen.

If it is a bull kudu that means horns and all. If you have to drive at night then keep scanning the verges on both sides of the roads for reflective eyes. Better still, don't drive at night.

Kudu raid crops and apparently happily will eat tobacco plants - I have no idea if they chew and spit or just swallow. They are popular for leather products e.g. kudu leather armchairs. The tannery at Swakopmund does a nice line (lines in fact) in kudu leather shoes, hats and belts.

In the late seventies rabies broke out amongst the large Namibian kudu population. The disease spread on average 60 km per year across the country and thousands of kudu died. By the early 1980's over 50% of the kudus were estimated to have died. Coming from Europe I tend to think of rabies as being spread by things with sharp teeth like foxes and dogs. The reality is that it also occurs in animals with grinding teeth like cattle. The virus is transmitted through saliva. In many parts of the world rabies has a species that acts as a maintenance population for the virus. Depending on the region it could be jackals, bat-eared foxes, meerkats or dogs. With all these species you can see that their carnivorous nature could allow the spread of the virus through saliva infection when they bite things. While I like the idea of rabid kudu chasing animals and trying to bite them, this seems rather improbable. So how does rabies spread with kudus? One suggestion is that as they browse the thorny bushes in the Namibian countryside they leave saliva behind on the thorns. This saliva is then picked up by another kudu who browses on the same thorny bush a little later.

Kudus have a routine to their fighting. The horns interlock in a specific way then they try to push the other guy over. The horns can grow to 180cm in length. Normally they have two and a half rotations, occasionally three. Have a look at any big males you see and try to count the revolutions in the horns - I find it tricky, some sort of optical illusion on my eyes? On rare occasions two males kudus have been found dead joined together by their locked horns.

Springbok

Namibia's gazelle is plentiful across most of the country. In places like Etosha your eyes start to screen them out when scanning a horizon looking for other less common game. However what we see now is a remnant of what they once were. Springbok are famous for their great migrations. Herds of thousands would move across places like the Kalahari. According to one author they went to the sea once, drank the water and died leaving thousands of bodies washed up along the beach. Historical accounts describe herds numbering millions of animals. These days their numbers are smaller and there are things like fences to deal with so you don't see the great migrations.

Springbok are willing to move in search of good food. They both browse and graze which provides them with more opportunities to feed. They do not need to drink every day, and even when they do drink they seem able to drink very heavily mineralized water that other animals find undrinkable. All this makes for animals you can still see in high densities at places like Etosha. A good game to play while driving round Etosha in the midday sun is "How many springbok can hide from the sun under one tree?". Little groups will occupy every bit of shade under a tree or large bush. Try counting them to see what your record is.

Why do Springbok pronk? Pronking is the jumping up in the air they are famous for. Various theories exist, equating pronking to fitness displays. Most of the pronking is done by young animals and an entertaining theory is that they do it to see better. Springbok have large eyes and the 2 metre jumps in the air give them a better view of the flat area they inhabit, allowing them to see landmarks for navigation. After moving long distances in search of food they will rapidly home (like pigeons) when rains appear. This ability to home requires good navigation which the younger animals need to learn, but the older animals have already learnt - hence they pronk less. I guess if this theory is correct then pronking should slowly reduce as the ability for springbok to migrate reduces and they become confined to game farms.

Springbok are one of those species whose Latin name tells you something about the animal. In Latin they are called Antidorcas marsupialis. Why marsupialis? Marsupials are animals with pouches, like kangaroos and wombats. Springbok have a pouch, it's just not for babies. The pouch runs along the far end of their back. It can open to reveal a white dorsal crest. Both this crest and the white buttock hair can be raised in display. The pouch walls also secrete a scent to add to the display signal.

Springbok are popular game farm animals. Even in places like Etosha you will find springbok stew on the menu. Game farming has had its impact on the springbok. There is now a variety of black springbok. Farmers have been breeding from springbok that have chocolate black skin all over and a white blaze down the nose. A bit like white tigers, they are beautiful but what does it do to the species to breed up these unnatural characteristics? In the competition between game lodges having wild black springbok on your land is another way to get the tourists to visit your lodge rather than your neighbors. Farmers are also selectively breeding bigger springbok. At what point does the African experience become unnatural? Conversely would you rather have Africa full of introduced cattle, or endemic but selectively bred Springbok?

Buffalo

I know lots of people are scared of domestic cows. What then would they feel about the wild african buffalo? Buffalo belong to the big five club along with elephants and lions. Some people claim that buffalo are the most dangerous animal to hunt. Once you see them, especially a bull, you start to believe it. They just look so solid, any rugby team would be proud to have a few on their side. Buffalo are widespread across Africa but fairly rare in Namibia. They need shade and water, two things Namibia is not famous for. This restricts them to the Caprivi with some attempts to establish a population at the Waterberg plateau. They don't like the midday sun, and are particularly active at night when it is cooler. If you want to see them in places like Mahango it is best to arrive at sunrise when they can often be seen going into the swamp for the day. It is thought that buffalo originally lived in forests (as their cousin the forest buffalo does today). They came out of the forest and grew bigger, but still retain some of the physiology from their forest days, including poor vision but good hearing. Most long time savannah inhabitants have good vision.

Buffalo are associated with diseases like rinderpest. In the 1890's they were hunted out of parts of Namibia following an outbreak of rinderpest. None of the Namibian game farms and lodges keeps buffalo. I believe this is because of the threat from disease they pose to domestic livestock. This always seems a shame since buffalo are happy eating old and new grass. They can clear away the old grass so other fussier animals are then able to feed as well. They seem better suited to the African lifestyle than the domestic cows. Maybe a sign of true commitment to game farming will be when buffalo become widespread.

Hartebeest

Hartebeest are curious in that you could classify them as ugly or attractive according to your mood. They have the flat thin faces with shortish horns that always seem popular in films about supernatural horned people.

There are two sorts of hartebeest in Namibia. The common red hartebeest, and the rarer tsessebe. Their status partly reflects their diet and lifestyle. The red can go without water, and will browse as well as graze. The tsessebe must have water, and just grazes. So you get the tsessebe in similar places to the sable i.e. the North East parks along the Caprivi. Tsessebe also occur in western parts of Etosha and on the Waterberg plateau. Both places where they have been introduced by people. There are lots of other sorts of hartebeest in Africa, (wildebeest are closely related), and many people consider the tsessebe to be a subspecies of the topi that occurs further north and beyond into East Africa.

Somehow it does not look that way but Hartebeest are some of the fastest animals on the plains. Tsessebe can outrun predators by running at speeds of up to 65 km/hr.

When looking at a Hartebeest you might ask "Why the long faces?" Instead ask yourself why the short necks and you will have the answer. Given most of their food is grass and that they are fairly tall, they can either get a long neck, or a long face, to help them reach the ground. I guess that short necks allow you to go faster than long necks (a personal intuition rather than scientific conclusion) and if you are living in reasonably open places then speed helps.

There is one other hartebeest that needs to be mentioned. It is the bontebok. This very attractive antelope is not native to Namibia but many of the game lodges and farms have them. Like the black wildebeest they are another South African species that came close to extinction. In the 1930's they were down to about 30 individuals. Their numbers have increased since then and they are now pretty widespread thanks to game farming. They represent one of the dilemmas of using game farming as a conservation tool; you save an endangered species but in the process disturb the balance by saving it in the wrong places e.g introduce an alien species. Currently people are discussing bringing tigers to South Africa to help conserve them. If it is okay to introduce antelopes to areas that were not part of their original geographic range then some people may also consider introducing tigers to Africa defensible.

Giraffe

The giraffe's name comes from an Arabic word meaning creature of grace (the translation seems to vary by author but this one works for me). This is a perfect description of them walking. However it is all surface deep, surprise one and they look really worried with legs and necks going everywhere and loosing any grace until their brain has caught up. The grace partly comes from the relatively peculiar way they walk, first both left legs, then both right legs in a sort of rolling gait. Most other animals do opposite legs together which reduces the rolling.

Namibia has the Angolan sub-species of giraffe. They occur naturally across the North of the country and Etosha has a good population. They are fairly popular on game farms so you may come across them anywhere - the main road 30 km north of Windhoek often gives views of the large herd at Okapuka. A small population lives alongside some of the desert elephants in the Hoanib flood-plain (a slightly ironic name I always feel). These desert giraffes often go without drinking and seem to get their moisture from plants, both internally and externally due to the dew (try saying that out loud).

The fun trivia fact about giraffes is that they have the same number of bones in their neck as we do in ours (seven). They are just very big bones. They are the largest ruminants, which means they chew the cud so any food eaten goes up and down that long neck a number of times. They use their necks for fighting and have been known to knock over an eland with a good neck hit. Long necks put giraffes in the upmarket vegetarian section of African society (pun intended). Eating plants can be tough stuff with a lot of digestive capacity required to get nutrition out of them. Think of the size of an elephant, rhino, or buffalo - and how much of this is their stomach. Then look at a Giraffe, their stomach is comparatively small given it has to feed one of the largest mammals in the world. This is because they get good, high quality food at the tops of the trees. Less work is required to break it down for absorption by their gut. The rhinos and elephants eat poorer quality food so need more of it, and hence have proportionally bigger stomachs.

For their size giraffes, like elephants, are masters of blending into the bush. In any area with scrub or trees if you find one giraffe, congratulate yourself, then try and spot another near by. This process can continue for a while until you have found over a dozen scattered around the area (actually thirty two is my record). They seem to handle hilly habitat surprisingly well, and because of this you can find yourself driving along and suddenly see a giraffes head at the same height as your own. Theory has it that the need to eat a lot, the protection coming from their large size, and their ability to see across good distances all contribute to the dispersed nature of giraffe herds. There is no real social structure to giraffe society so you can get herds of mixed sex or single sex.

Giraffes develop bony structures on the top of their heads, including over their eyes (a bit like bone created eyebrows that shelter the eye from the elements). This makes them unable to look upwards, but then again at that height why would they need to look upwards?

For mothers reading this consider the giraffe's pregnancy which is just over four hundred and fifty days i.e. a year and a quarter. Some other impressive statistics are related to its circulatory system that needs to pump blood all the way up to the head. To manage this giraffe have a massive heart that has walls 7 cm thick and weighs a couple of percent of the overall body weight of the animal.

You can sex a giraffe by the hairiness of their horns. The females have tufts of hair on top, but the males have rubbed all their hair off making them bald. Of course size also helps for sexing - males are bigger than females. Both these methods only work for adults.

As you walk in the bush you come across many droppings made by antelopes. Though not an antelope, giraffe droppings have a similar shape and appearance but are a bit bigger (but not as big as you would expect). Kudu and eland droppings are nearly as big. Of course giraffe dropping fall from a great height compared those from kudu and eland, so if you are not sure who made the pile look at how scattered the pile is. Giraffe droppings will be scattered over a much wider area than an antelope's droppings.

Elephant

If there is a star animal in Namibia, the elephant must be it. Biggest land animal in the world, intelligent, strong social structure, and bound up in the politics of conservation. And if you want to see elephants, Namibia is a great place to do it. Namibian elephants are some of the biggest in

Africa. They are bush elephants, larger than their forest cousins - up to 4 metres high and over 6000 kg in weight.

Namibia has around nine to ten thousand elephants. There are three centers of elephant watching in the country. In the west you have the small but famous population of desert elephants. Around seven hundred animals spread over an area of 48000 sq km. People have argued about the taxonomic status of these animals, but the conclusion seems to be that they are bush elephants with long legs and big feet. They travel large distances up and down the river beds that run down to the sea. They have clever tricks to find water like sticking their trunks down their throat into their stomach and sucking liquid out. Places like Palmwag have regular visits from desert elephants.

Next there is the Etosha population. At one time elephants were extinct in Etosha. Occasional groups would pass through on their travels. A survey in the 1950's found only 26 animals! At this point a plan was devised to dig a series of boreholes over a 200 km line to attract elephants back into the park. By the 1980's the population numbered a few thousand and today they are a common resident in the park. At some of the waterholes south east of Okaukujeo you can see over a hundred at any one time. Given their size and population people find it frustrating at times that elephants can sometimes be difficult to see. An elephant can easily hide in a scrubby patch of bush. Worse still every summer (December of course given that Namibia is below the equator) the Etosha elephants move off to the North West of the park to enjoy the rains and the new vegetation it produces. This means you can easily visit Etosha and see no elephants! A severe disappointment.

Elephants do seem to take a perverse pleasure in scaring other animals away from waterholes. At times when they have youngsters this is possibly understandable, though a little over the top when it is a springbok they are scaring away. But at times you will find some individuals who just resent anyone else sharing their bath room with them.

In an ironic twist, the Etosha elephants may be the biggest in Africa, but they also have some of the shortest tusks. The belief is that the poor minerals in the area, and hence in their diet, cause the tusks to often break off. When watching elephants see if you can work out whether they are left or right tusked. The tusk they use most tends to be the shorter tusk.

Groups of elephants in the park have been killed in the past to try and limit the perceived damage they do when numbers get large.

Elephants can still be good wanderers and solitary males may leave the park and head off on a walkabout. Along with other animals like lions they can often turn up on the farms around Etosha and the wilder areas north west of the park.

The final major group of elephants is in the Caprivi. Until recently the Caprivi Strip was a military area. Much of the wildlife here has been heavily reduced but elephants seem to have managed to hang on, or have rapidly reoccupied it from neighboring Botswana. Mahango Park at the western end of Caprivi has the unusual property of being a sort of elephant bachelor pad. It seems to just hold males rather than the large matriarchal groups of females and young.

As you drive through the Caprivi heading east road signs warn of elephants crossing. Dropping on the road are large and you worry about whether to drive over or round them. This is the one place in Namibia where elephant urine regularly meets tarmac giving great big dark marks on the tarmac to accompany their big brown footballs. Fresh droppings are always a good sign of elephant activity in an area. Suddenly a herd of fifty individuals can appear through the trees and start crossing the road - so take care. In the times of conflict it was rumored that land mines would be hidden in the piles of elephant droppings on the road along the Caprivi strip.

At the end of the Caprivi you have the parks, swamps and rivers that border Chobe Park in Botswana. Botswana has over one hundred thousand elephants. Chobe is one of the great elephant reserves of Africa and in the summer many elephants leave the park and head north into Namibia. The Zambezi River is much lower at this time of year and you can see the elephants coming out to drink in pools along the river bed. Other places like the Golden Triangle south of Kongola also provide great elephant and water viewing. Elephants clearly love water and watching babies playing in it, or large bulls swimming a river, is one of the great pleasures Namibia can give you.

Conflict between man and elephant is not as great as in some parts of the world, but there is still conflict. Elephants raid crops, and on occasion kill people. In particular the Caprivi population faces such problems. Namibia is currently allowed to sell some stockpiled ivory to help fund elephant conservation. When you watch elephants ask yourself the question how will they survive and coexist with man in the years to come? Will they become doomed to living in parks and being managed, or is it ever possible for such large animals to be a part of the landscape beyond the park borders?

One of the recent discoveries about elephants is that they communicate using infrasound. This is low frequency noise that the elephant makes and it can carry for over 4km. A female elephant becomes receptive for mating on only a few days, often after a period of years! This gives her a very small time window in which to meet up with a male elephant and mate. Trying to find a good male must be even harder. One of the many uses of infrasound is to advertise a females availability widely in the area. In particular males in musth (a form of sexual heat) respond quickly to hearing the call. You just wonder if some forms of machinery emitting low frequency noises would attract sexually active male elephants - but it seems this is a rich and complex communication rather than a basic frequency response.

Hippopotamus

You only get hippos in the north east Caprivi starting from the waters where the strip meets the rest of Namibia. Places like the Kavango river that includes Popa falls and runs next to the Mahango Park. You get more hippos further east in the swamps at the far end of Caprivi and in the rivers bordering Zambia and Botswana. In many places the hippos have been hunted out, either for meat, or for pleasure. During the military times up along the Angolan border many people had boats with outboards and guns. Harassing and shooting hippos was one way some people passed their time. Hippos are already famous for being aggressive on occasion, but activities like this must have increased their belligerence to people and boats.

When cruising rivers like the Zambezi you may at first believe there are no hippos, but every so often you can see a large path leading out of the water where the hippos leave to go grazing for the night. If you meet a hippo at night don't get between him (or her) and the water. Remember they can go very fast. One of those useful/useless things to remember when protecting yourself from a charging hippo is that they can't jump and so don't like going over obstacles. What you think of an obstacle may not be what a hippo thinks, but other than that you should enjoy the moment. Hippos always seem bigger than you expect and seeing one up close makes you realise just how enormous these animals are. The other sign of hippos is the noise they make. You may often hear one before seeing one. They have the most magnificent bellow that has to be one of the defining sounds of Africa.

Hippos are not closely related to rhinos. A nice way to see this is with their footsteps - hippos are even toed, like pigs and antelopes, whereas rhinos are odd toed like horses. So when you go for a walk in a hippo area you may find two paths side by side with big four-toed footprints. The footprints look a bit like a maple leaf. The reason there are two paths together is because hippos are so wide that each side's feet creates its own path. Hippos can walk a long way at night; they have been seen wandering the streets of towns and villages, including places like Katima Mulilo, the capital of the Caprivi region.

Hippos are well suited to life in the water. They can sleep underwater, coming up to breathe while snoozing. The young can suckle underwater, again coming up every few minutes to breathe.

There is a nice story about hippos. When God created the world the hippos asked if they could live in the water because they enjoyed its coolness so much. God was worried though, he had already given the job of river predator to the crocodiles. He looked at the hippo's large mouth and big teeth and feared the hippo would eat all the fish in the rivers and lakes. The hippo pleaded with God to be allowed to live in the water. Eventually God said yes on one condition. They must never eat any fish, just stick to eating grass and other vegetation. The hippo agreed, and so to this day they regularly show God they have not eaten any fish. They do this by firstly flicking their dung everywhere with their little tails. This way God can see there are no fish bones in the droppings. Secondly, when sitting in the river they open their mouths wide to the sky to show God there are no fish in their mouths. Lastly they always come out of the river at night so God need not worry they are eating fish in the dark when he can not see them.

Hippos used to be hunted for their meat and ivory. The ivory is meant to be better than elephant ivory. Hunters had a special drum with a stick attached to its middle. By wetting your hand and pulling it along the stick you could make the drum vibrate giving a deep sound like a hippo calling. A hippo hearing this would assume another hippo was having a good feast and come out of the water to investigate, at which point the hunters would jump out with spears and kill the hippo.

Honey Badger (or Ratel)

Often called the most ferocious animal in Africa, these guys just seem to have personality. They sort of represent the grizzly bear of Africa, and have associated folklore and behaviour to go with it. Short sighted, snuffling, and digging round the bush, a slightly funny walk, and aggression by the bucket when required. If you want to see a honey badger then Namibia has to be one of the best places to try, but it won't be as easy as finding a zebra. Honey badgers are mainly nocturnal, though sometimes come out during daylight hours. A significant number of people see them in Etosha. They can sometimes be seen in places with nocturnal game watching activities e.g Okonjima south of Otjiwarongo - home of the AfriCat foundation. It is also worth checking low bushes with chanting goshawks sitting on them. The goshawks follow the badgers to catch things the badgers disturb.

Honey badgers really do like honey. Their Latin genus name Mellivora translates roughly to 'devourer of honey'. They do indeed work with the honey guide birds to find and break open bees nests. Honey badgers live dangerously and happily eat snakes, whether they are poisonous or not. If you see a honey badger meet a puff adder, put your money on the badger. Like skunks, honey badgers have anal sacs that can eject a foul smelling substance. Given their lack of fear and ability to take on all comers the sacs would not seem to be required for defense. Some people believe the fluid in the sacs is used to get rid of the bees around a bee hive that the badger is breaking into. The honey badger sprays the foul fluid round using his tail and sometimes while performing a handstand to gain height. Bee keepers have reported piles of dead bees with a foul smell at hives that honey badgers have dinned at.

The other famous rumor about the honey badger is that when he (or she) attacks, she will go for the groin. A famous African ornithologist once reckoned a cricketing cup and jock strap is what you should wear if working with honey badgers. Stories are told of groin attacks on animals as large as buffalo with the buffalo then bleeding to death. Given they are considerably shorter than a buffalo it would seem inevitable to me that some form of groin attack would be part of any fight. Curiously the honey badger, proportionally speaking, has one of the largest brains of any carnivore so maybe attacking the groin is part of some intelligent master plan developed over the years. They also have exceptionally large testicles. Given they regularly come under attack from bees and ants this would seem to be a disadvantage but it might also explain their aggressive nature.

Small Monkeys

Namibia is fairly poor in primates with only the baboon, the vervet monkey and the lesser bushbaby occurring. The vervet and bushbaby are restricted to the north of the country. Vervets are active by day and bushbabies by night. A nocturnal wander with a torch around the grounds of a lodge like De la Bat at Waterberg is the way to find bushbabies. Walk along the road around the luxury bungalows, but don't go into the bushes since they may have snakes. Dusk is the best time when the bushbabies are starting to appear and there is still just enough light to see their shadows as they move between the branches. Listen out for a twittering call and watch for a small pair of reflected yellow eyes amongst the thorn trees (hold your torch next to your head to see the eye reflection easier). When watching them move around the trees remember a Bushbaby can leap over twenty times its body length, crossing gaps of a couple of meters.

The Namibian vervet is famous for having paler hands and feet than their relatives elsewhere in Africa. All vervets have comparatively small thumbs that make a static rather than mobile diet easier for them e.g. gathering fruit and seeds rather than catching insects. Vervets are active at the hottest parts of the day and seem able to take heat well. Studies of vervets elsewhere in Africa have shown them to have comparatively complex calls e.g. they have one danger call for eagles above, and a different call for snakes on the ground. Mahango Park is a nice place to watch troops of vervets.

Vervet society is all about hierarchy. You can use the angle of a vervets tail to measure how confident or submissive he is feeling. Up and curved over the back makes you the coolest monkey on the savannah. Horizontally straight back parallel to the ground means you need counseling. A "male only" display of confidence and power is to show off your red and blue genitals.

Baboon

Your first sight of a baboon in Namibia will probably be on a road as you travel round the country. Most of the roads into and out of Windhoek are well guarded by baboons. If you fail to see them there then many of the lodges in the parks will have a baboon troop nearby ready to raid the bins and steal food. The worse thing you can do is feed them or leave food easily accessible for them. At Waterberg the baboons are professional chalet breakers. They will enter through an open bathroom window, defecate everywhere inside the bungalow, ransack all possible food items, and finally make off with any good prizes.

Baboons are powerful animals. When people take their dogs walking at Avis Dam near Windhoek the braver/stupider dogs will try and chase the baboons. The local vet has a good business sewing up dogs with large gashes and cuts that have inflicted on the dogs by the baboons. The baboons round Avis Dam even come visiting the town. People living in houses adjoining the dam can enter their sitting room to find a baboon at the fruit bowl helping himself! A little time back a baboon got as far as the centre of Windhoek. The story I was told was that he first went to the Ministry of Home Affairs building, from there he moved on to the Ministry of Foreign Affairs, before ending up at the Parliament building. Here it was established he could not vote, so alas he was shot.

Baboons are viewed as pests in Namibia and may be shot. They raid crops and even take young goats and sheep. Farmers readily shoot them. There is a dilemma when out walking - you want to stay inconspicuous and quiet, but in many places there are people out hunting. Last year a tourist out bird watching was shot by a farmer out hunting baboons. It was a tragic mistake and the farmer only found out the error after he sent one of his farm hands to check the baboon's body. This is another reason to make sure you tell your hosts when you go off for a walk in the bush, just in case they know people are out hunting.

Baboons are used by many shyer animals as a security system. After the baboons have arrived at a waterhole other species will follow relying on the excellent security system baboons have to detect predators.

Baboons make curious foot prints. Most animals have similar front and back footprints since the front and back 'paws' are both feet. Baboons have hands rather than feet at the front, and when walking only part of the hand touched the ground to leave a print. All of the back feet touch the ground so baboons leave behind two different sorts of footprint.

Given their widespread distribution and adaptability I still find it amazing that there are no baboons in the Etosha Park. In fact the park lacks any monkeys. Unlike Waterberg and other parks you need not worry about baboon theft. Their need for water and cliffs or large trees to sleep in is known to restrict the baboon empire. Etosha has waterholes, but not many cliffs, so is it that the trees are just not big enough for them.

Warthog

Along with kudu and elephant, the warthog has managed to get its own Namibian road sign. Warthogs are not that big but they are very tough. They can cause major damage to any car that hits them (or they hit!). A big strong skull and massive teeth coming out that can happily puncture a car radiator. I suspect warthogs have the attitude that if you are going to take them down, they will do their best to take you down with them. This toughness seems to pass through to other aspects of their life. They look tough and on occasion will readily take on a leopard or other predator that fails to catch them by surprise. They have a habit of breaking fences that get in their way. Their hide makes good leather. Big tusks on the males have been recorded growing up to 40 cm long in Namibia. On many game lodge walls you will see pairs of warthog tusks mounted as trophies.

You can tell male and female warthogs apart by the number of "warts" on their face. The male has four and the female has two. The warts are not really warts of course; they are made up of skin and tissue. A group of warthogs is called a sounder of warthogs. They normally spend the night in a burrow. They enter the burrow backwards so that their defensive tusks face the entrance and can ward of predators. The belief is that old and injured warthogs often die in their burrow which is why you don't often find warthog bodies in the bush. Warthog and aardvark holes are the curse of cross country bush drivers since they are big enough for a wheel to "fall" into. Warthogs can dig their own burrows but prefer to take over an old aardvark or porcupine burrow, and then reshape it to their taste. Livestock on farms (like calves) have been lost by falling into warthog burrows and people, especially children, are easily able to get inside a warthog burrow. Please don't try this with your own children.

The burrows work as a sort of guesthouse system. All the warthogs in an area will happily use any burrow. If a burrow is occupied they just find another one. Clever lions have been known to spend the night sniffing burrows to see which ones are occupied and then wait in hiding next to the burrow entrance for the warthog to appear in the morning - bacon for breakfast.

Warthogs lack any real fur and a significant part of their life is devoted to trying to manage their body temperature. They use their deep burrows to escape extremes of temperature. You will often see warthogs lying down together to conserve heat, and they like sunbathing to warm up. Where they can find it (not many places in Namibia) they use mud to cool themselves down. After a mud bath warthogs suffer from the same problem as rhinos. Namely their necks are too short and bodies to fat to easily scratch themselves all over so they rub themselves on trees and stones instead. You will often see dry mud sticking to the lower trunk of tree near places where warthogs (and rhinos) go to wallow.

Warthogs have one un-pig like habit. The way they lie down and stand up. Pigs, like dogs, sit down by first lowering their bottom and then their forelegs. Warthogs do the same as antelopes and deer, they lower their forelegs first and then their hind legs. Getting up is the reverse of lying down.

One question I have not yet found the answer to is why you rarely get warthog on the various game menus at restaurants and lodges in Namibia. The animals are plentiful and the meat is good (it is pork after all). What stops it being covered in sauce? One reason might be that warthogs will happily feed on carrion if they can find it.

You do get another species of pig up in the Caprivi - the bushpig. Differences between the two species are that the bushpig is nocturnal, is hairy, and runs with his tail down. The warthog is diurnal (daytime), lacks any body hair, and runs with his tail up.

Dolphins and Whales

Namibia used to be a popular location for whale hunters. You can still find evidence of their communities along the Namibian coast e.g. at South Sandwich. Whales pretty well disappeared from Namibian waters and are only just starting to return. If you want to be sure to see whales you are better off going down to Cape Town in South Africa. If you are willing to settle for whale bones then traveling in the Skeleton Coast Park should make you happy. Remember it is a park and you can not take home any bones you find.

You do have a good chance of seeing dolphins in Namibia (well Namibian waters). A family of bottle-nosed dolphins is resident in the waters between Walvis Bay and Swakopmund. They often swim right next to the shore (like 5 meters from the beach) to avoid the large ships further offshore. Tracking them down may be tricky, so to improve your chances take one of the dolphin and seal boat cruises from Walvis Bay or Long Beach. Otherwise watch the sea from the Strand at Swakopmund. They often appear in the small bay there or going past the promentary at the bay entrance. Dolphins no longer have the high moral ground image they used to. Studies have shown they bully, commit rape, and have all the other human traits we get embarrassed by.

The waters off Namibia hold species other than bottle nosed dolphin. Heaviside's dolphin is a local specialty being mainly restricted to the cold Benguela current. The large coastal seal colonies attract killer whales. A visit to the Cape Cross colony in August gives you one of the better chances of seeing them

Water Antelopes of the Caprivi

Namibia, land of desert and no rain, yet the most aquatic antelopes in the world occur here. The top right of Namibia borders the Okavango swamps. Namibia has its own, fairly unknown swamps that form part of this watery world. In them you find the red lechwe, reedbuck, bushbuck, puku, waterbuck and the sitatunga, all water loving antelopes. Sitatunga inhabit the deepest sections of the swamps and have special hooves to enable them to travel in this watery world. As the land gets drier you will encounter red lechwe, reedbuck and puku, then waterbuck and bushbuck. The waterbuck and puku only occur at the far end of the Caprivi, and sitatunga in the wet areas bordering Botswana. The parks of Mahango, Mamili and Mudumu in the Caprivi should be visited to see these animals. Apart from the parks, the lodges along the far eastern end of the Namibia and Botswana border should be visited.

Waterbuck occur on some of the game farms. They are popular with hunters and photographers so tend to occur in habitats that are rather unnatural for them e.g. game lodges near Windhoek hundreds of kilometers from any natural watery swamp. You need to be careful when skinning a Waterbuck for its meat since they have a very strong smell. This comes from an oily secretion on their fur. Even people are able to smell it some time after a Waterbuck has left a location. If skinned badly the smell can contaminate the meat making it rather unpalatable. There is some discussion as to whether predators like lions also find the smell repugnant, since there are records of them leaving waterbuck kills only partially eaten. An ironic statistic is that lions often have a higher than average success rate killing waterbuck compared to other items of prey. Presumably this is because waterbuck smell so strongly and are therefore easier to find. Waterbuck have little fear of crocodile infested waters and some people believe the pungent smell discourages crocodiles from killing them. Do we really believe that crocodiles are fussy about the smell of their food.

Many of these antelope's lives are controlled by the rivers they frequent. The lechwe live on the grassy river plains bordering the rivers. As the rivers rise and fall so do the areas the lechwe live in.

The end of the Caprivi is a sort of meeting point in Africa. The deserts further south west are finishing, mighty African rivers like the Zambezi pass by, swamps like the Okavango block your way. For many of the species found further north this is a southern most outpost of their range. Puku and waterbuck are examples of this. They are widespread further north and east but this represents their south west limit.

Unlike the hartebeest and other antelopes from drier areas none of these aquatic antelopes have speed on their side when evading predators. Hiding and water play large part of their defense. Sitatunga spend large amounts of time submerged in the waters of thick papyrus swamps. Waterbuck will enter water to evade predators. Lechwe have feet that are adapted to moving comparatively fast over soft swampy ground which predators may find difficult to run over, plus they live in grassy areas with little cover to allow predators to get close. Bushbuck are masters of camouflage. They retire to thickets, but also bed down at night in the open where they seem relatively invisible to predators. Lions have been seen walking within 10 meters of a bushbuck that is hiding this way.

Wildebeest

Wildebeest are also called gnu (how do you do). They used to be more plentiful in Namibia. Currently if you go to Etosha you may be forgiven for thinking they still are, but both the Etosha population and many of the areas outside Etosha have lower populations than they once had (or none at all). At one time over twenty five thousand used to migrate through Etosha and the top left corner of Namibia. Fences round

Etosha, hunting, and drought years that caused animals to move north to Angola rather than return to Etosha have all contributed to the wildebeest's decline. The road building program in Etosha also had an impact on the wildebeest population. The authorities dug large amounts of gravel out of the ground to create the excellent roads in Etosha. The resulting gravel pits collected water and became breeding grounds for anthrax in the park. At the time this killed around three quarters of the park's wildebeest.

Wildebeest are dependant on water and only occur within 15 to 20 km of it. They are also pure grazers needing short grass. In this respect they can be dependant on other grazers like zebras to clear the bush for them. So if you look at an area with lots of grass but no wildebeest then check how long the grass is, it may be too long for wildebeest to live there. This need for short grass and water is what makes them migratory, and is why the fencing of Etosha (and other areas in Africa) has caused them such problems.

Wildebeest live in herds and the herds collect together to form bigger groups. Wildebeest are fairly slow animals compared to their cousins like hartebeest. Wildebeest can be outrun by most large predators so the herd behavior helps defend them. The slight irony of all this is that when you see a wildebeest you normally see a lot of wildebeest. People think they are common, but you either get a lot or none at all. This "all or nothing" nature means that in some respects the wildebeest is an animal on a slippery slope to extinction since unlike many other antelopes such as kudu, wildebeest can now only survive in large protected and managed areas i.e. they will only live on in large national parks and their abundance is an illusion created by a few large concentrations.

Most baby wildebeest arrive in November and December. The calves are rather smart animals compared to their shaggy parents. On average calves can run within 7 minutes of birth, and after two days can keep up with the adults. The ungainly proportions of the wildebeest seem to suit the adolescents giving them the slightly ungainly appearance of human adolescent youngsters. You can age the animals by their horn development. They take three years to reach their adult state. Two year old horns look like smaller versions of their parents horns. Short, nearly straight horns, will be this years youngsters. If they still have their tan hide then they will only be a month or two old.

At night wildebeest are said to settle down in columns i.e. a line one after the other. Given you can not drive round Etosha at night I can not confirm this. Why do they do it? - the theory is that columns allow you to stay as a group but you can get up and run away fast without bumping into each other.

Namibia has one native wildebeest, the blue wildebeest which is also called the brindled gnu. This is the same species as its northern cousin the white bearded wildebeest that occurs in East Africa. Just to make life confusing many of the game farms have the other species of wildebeest which is not native to Namibia. This is the black wildebeest also known as the white tailed gnu. A smaller, smarter animal. If you are trying to remember which name matches which gnu then avoid using the blue and black. Blue is just a silly name. Blue is very rare amongst mammals. How many blue mammals can you name? Many blue wildebeest look pretty black, especially the males on a sunny day under a dark tree. Brindled (referring to the brown streaks down the neck) and white tailed are much more of a 'what you see is what they are' name. The white tailed gnu was once reduced to only a few hundred individuals, but now has a world wide population of thousands and growing, thanks to game ranches.

Impala

Namibia has two sorts of impala, the common, and the black-faced Impala. In Namibian terms the black-faced may qualify as the normal sort, but in terms of southern Africa and the world they are a localised minority. The common impala (technically the sub species melampus) has the widespread distribution, but within Namibia they only occur naturally in the Caprivi strip. The reason you may see them elsewhere is that they are cheaper and easier to buy than the rarer black-faced impala whose natural range is the north-west corner of Namibia. Cheaper you ask? People who farm and display game often want to have a large variety of game on their land. If you have twenty species of mammal on your land and your neighbor only has ten there is a good chance more tourists will visit you. So there is a healthy trade in game between game farms in southern Africa. You can buy most species and like any market the rare ones cost more. So farmers buying game tend to buy the common impala. Over time some escape from the game farms and the worry is that they may meet up with the wild black-faced impala and start to breed with them. This could bring about the genetic extinction of the black-faced impala subspecies.

Why did a separate subspecies evolve in western Namibia? A view is that a lack of water between the black-faced in the west and the common populations in the Caprivi has acted as an impenetrable barrier. This has allowed the black faced to develop their pretty black blaze down their forehead.

In the 1960's the black-faced impala were considered endangered and over 250 of them were captured and moved to the Etosha Park. Impala tend to stay in a small area for life so do not spread fast into new areas. The Etosha group bred well but individuals had to be moved to other parts of the park to help them spread out and increase their numbers. They are now widely spread round Etosha and some have been sold to game farmers.

Impala are the only antelopes to have scent glands on their fetlocks (ankles in effect). These seem to be used to mark paths as they walk along them. Also the scent may be given off when they kick their legs up in the air. Theory says the scent is used to help groups find each other, but given the highly sedentary nature of impala and fairly weak social structure they seem to have I am unclear how likely this theory is.

The rutting season for impala is short and the males spend the whole time chasing females and fighting off rivals. They get so exhausted by this that they may only be able to hold a territory for days, or maybe a week or two before another male takes over their patch.

One secret of the impala's success in Africa is that unlike many antelopes they can be both a browser and a grazer. This makes them able to survive changes in food supply. Despite their athletic looking build they are not fast animals. For predator avoidance tactics they rely on the cover of the bush along with their ability to jump up to 3 meters into the air.

Assuming you can tell impala dropping from any other antelope droppings, how can you tell what sex made the droppings? One clue is the spacing between droppings. Female impala squat down at the rear when defecating and this leaves a fairly tidy pile. Male impala do not squat down so the droppings fall from a greater height and tend to give a more scattered disperse arrangement to their droppings.

Mongoose

These guys get everywhere. In particular the yellow mongoose is very common in urban areas. You see them all round Windhoek. On occasion you even put your foot in their droppings while walking round town or home. Most evening they turn up to see what food people have dropped in their outdoor dining area. Their cousins the slender mongoose will happily wondering into an empty kitchen with an open door. Normally you see the slender mongoose on the roads as you drive round the country. They often carry their tails curled up and seem to have remarkably hairy tails - on occasion you might just mistake them for a ground squirrel. To make it confusing the yellow mongoose has two color phases, the traditional (in my mind) yellow version with a white tip to its tail, and the grey version that is more rarely seen. The slender mongoose is a rich brown colour, often with a dark tip to its tail, and does look more slender should you have a yellow mongoose handy to compare it with.

Namibia also has plenty of film star mongooses, the meerkats or suricates. These guys have appeared in a number of popular natural history films. They go around in groups often with their tails held vertically up in the air. They like to sit upright on their hind legs watching for predators, and they have a fundamentally inquisitive nature. A number of the lodges have families of suricates that live round the buildings, and run between the table legs looking for anything that might be edible, or just chewable.

Meerkats run a tight early warning system. While foraging one member of the troop is always on guard from some lookout point. The guard will keep making quiet noises so that the troop knows that all is well. So silence means the guard is in trouble. The guard will sound a short bark for danger from the air, and a high pitched sound for danger on the ground.

Both suricates and yellow mongooses will quite often associate with ground squirrels and use ground squirrel burrows for their own homes.

There are a number of other Namibian mongoose species. The two other species you are most likely to come across are the banded and dwarf mongoose. Both look like their names and both live in groups. If you see a group of dwarf mongooses running away as you walk or drive, then stop and wait a few seconds. They normally can not help stopping to turn round and look back.

North east Namibia along the Caprivi has some of the more water loving species of mongoose. For example the large grey mongoose which occasionally travels as a family nose to tail, creating a larger, longer, virtual animal.

It is quite interesting to compare the lifestyles of three of the Namibian mongoose species; the suricate, yellow and banded mongooses.

They all like to construct warrens to live in. These can be large constructions e.g. suricate warrens have been recorded with over 90 entrances holes and going down to 3 meters in depth on a number of different levels.

Scent marking is also part of their community structure. In both yellow and banded mongooses all the pack members get scent marked by each other to create a group smell.

All three have a similar daily routine. They are active in the warm daylight hours. They rise and use the communal latrine. If it is not yet warm enough they will sunbathe, or return to bed. Once it is warm they will start foraging. Their techniques vary slightly here - suricates will go off as a reasonably tight group, banded mongooses that live in larger groups will go off in a more dispersed group. Yellow mongooses live in large colonies but go off as individuals or couples, which is why you never think of them as communal animals even though they are.

The banded mongooses are the guys who will take an egg (or millipede or beetle) and push it hard and fast between their back legs so it hits a rock and smashes allowing them to eat it. In terms of snake eating none of these guys are world masters, instead honey badgers and birds of prey are the real snake eaters.

Lion

Lions mainly occur in the north of Namibia. They also can be seen down south in the Kalahari areas bordering Botswana and South Africa e.g. next to the Kalahari Gemsbok National Park

Seeing lions is mainly done in Etosha. They occur in the other parks along the Caprivi and in Khaudum Game Park but access and viewing are not so easy. Lions do spread out from Etosha and individuals will head south and west into the farmlands. The Etosha park staff spend part of their time trying to chase them back into the park. Further to the west of Etosha there is a small population that lives in the Skeleton Coast.

To find lions you should spend a couple of days in Etosha. The waterhole at Okaukujeo often has visits from lions during the dryer months, especially at night. If you are hoping for a lion this way, then bear in mind that lions often just spend a few minutes at a waterhole, so leave the waterhole to go to the toilet or get a drink at your own risk. In daylight hours checking the waterholes round Etosha seems the best way to find them. There are certain waterholes that often have lions, or signs of lions e.g. Okandeka always seems to have the bodies of victims on display. If you visit a waterhole that seems suspiciously empty then be suspicious. Often you will find lions lying under a tree or bush somewhere near the water. They like the big bushes they can "get inside". At night you will often hear the lions roaring round the Etosha camps.

Lion kills are normally just eaten where the kill is made. They have no need to hide them. If you see bodies of zebras and other large herbivores that have been killed and eaten, they are probably lion or possibly hyena kills since leopards and cheetahs will move their kills to more sheltered and safer positions.

Lions are pretty well king of the beasts in Namibia, they can take young elephant and rhino as prey, and can easily steal food from other predators (see hyena section). They should be treated with respect. Attacks on people are not unknown. The rainy season is toughest for them since rather than concentrated round the waterholes their prey are widely scattered. During these times they have to be more imaginative in finding food. When times are hard for them they have been known to enter people's huts - presumably looking for food. Like the leopard they have been known to eat dogs, and evidence suggests the few lions along the skeleton coast may turn to hunting seals during such periods.

If you really must see a lion then visit some of the lodges down in the south east of Namibia that border the massive national park in Botswana and South Africa. Lions (and cheetahs) are often easier to see here.

Some of the lodges have captive lions and offer feeding "experiences" where you can get up close e.g. Mt Etjo, Okapuka. These can give impressive views of lions tearing away at a chained up hunks of meat two meters from your face. The left over bones of previous meals are often scattered all round, and such experiences may bring to mind the old Roman Games where Lions fought Gladiators. Don't assume they are just big domestic cats, on one occasion visitors had to witness the lion feeder becoming supper for his captives. People being killed by lions are pretty unusual but some time back an infamous incident occurred when a lion got into one of the Etosha camps at night and killed a camper sleeping out in the open.

Apart from the title 'King of the Beasts', lions also are up for a chance to win the mammal sexual marathon award. The females come into heat for about five days. During this time the male will mate with her about every 20 minutes. If his energy wanes the female will keep walking in front of him and rubbing her body on him until he performs. One of the theories for such intense mating is that it ensures the pride lion fathers the young, rather than some interloper who managed to nip in while the pride male was busy elsewhere. Male lions tend to kill cubs they do not think they have fathered.

A final observation on lions - while they are a must see animal and are wonderfully impressive when walking across a plain or coming down to a floodlit waterhole, for most of the time they are incredibly boring and just sleep. There is far more entertainment to be had in an elephant family at a waterhole.

Leopard

Leopard is another of the must see animals. Given its secretive nature this leaves many people disappointed or envious when they meet others who have been lucky enough to see one. In East Africa the tour guides have a good network that informs one another of where they have recently seen animals like leopard. This sort of network does not really exists in Namibian parks, but talking to people round the lodges, reading the lodge visitor sightings books, and talking to people you pass round the parks will all help you find things. Apart from in the extreme coastal desert leopards can be found all over Namibia. A few months back a leopard had taken up residence in one of the Windhoek suburbs and was taking dogs for it supper. This highlights the extremely flexible and successful nature of leopards. Where do you go to see one though? Maybe an all night watch at the Halali waterhole in Etosha will give you your best chance. Driving around in the early morning and late evening can also produce them.

It is difficult to explain just how good at hiding a leopard can be. I have seen people who keep leopards unable to find them in a 75 by 25 meter cage. Just as they are about to give up the leopard is found watching everyone from under a bush about 5 meters directly in front. The basic moral here is that leopards watch people rather than people watch leopards.

If you are willing to forgo the authentic wild experience then many of the game farms keep leopards. Dusternbrook just north of Windhoek probably has the most impressive show. You get driven into a series of large enclosures where meat is put out for the leopards. You are in an open jeep style car and the leopards get pretty close!

If you miss seeing a leopard then there is a good chance you may see the signs of a leopard. Their kills can be seen in trees as you drive round places like Etosha. Don't just look in the high trees. Springbok have been carried up what I would describe as bushes. One problem with looking for leopard kills is that leopards eat a wide range of food; Birds, rodents, dogs, jackals, hyrax, baboon, even insects. They are also known to develop individual tastes (or skills at catching?) so you may not get many kills in trees if your local leopard has a tendency for the smaller food items like hyrax.

Leopards can be extremely dangerous. They are respected by the Bushmen who tell you that the leopard waits in a tree to jump on you, then grabs you by the back of the neck and pulls your skin from there up over the top of your head, all the way over until it covers your eyes.

Unlike lions, leopards tend to move their large kills away from the place it was killed to a safer location, either under a bush or up a tree. For all their power leopards seems to have a healthy fear of other animals when challenged and can loose a kill to hyenas and lions, hence their wish to make it safer. Unlike some carnivores neither the lion nor the leopard will eat the stomach or intestines of their prey.

Canine

The canine family is the dog family. The black-backed jackal is probably going to be your first African "dog". They occur throughout Namibia - down at the coast trotting through the salt pans, or inland hanging around the waterholes at Etosha like ghosts. They are not popular with farmers since given the opportunity they will take young lambs. Black-backed jackals are considered more aggressive than their cousin the side-striped jackal. Some people believe the difference in aggressiveness is linked to their visibility. The side-striped has a fairly bland skin pattern, while the black-backed has a more visible high contrast pattern. The theory is that you are aggressive you can afford to be more visible to other animals.

Black-backed jackals like to deposit their droppings in prominent places, like on top of clumps of vegetation or rocks. Also they (along with hyenas) seem to like to eat the droppings of african wild dogs. Given wild dogs are already scarce, this reduces even further the chances of you finding a wild dog's droppings!

Side-striped always seems a bad name to me - the stripe is not obvious at a distance so linking what you see to what it is called never seems to work. Side-striped jackals have a preference for water which may explain their restricted range in Namibia. They are found in the north which is the wetter part of the country.

Unlike hyenas that carry food to cubs, members of the dog family will eat it, travel to their destination, and then regurgitate it for the cubs to eat. Another different solution to the same problem is when moving the cubs. Most predators like cats and mustelids will carry the youngsters in their mouth. Instead black-backed jackal mothers make the sound meaning a milk feed is available, but rather than sit down to feed, they just keep moving out of reach and so tempting the cubs to follow.

Leopards are very fond of a bit of dog meat and if they can find a young or old jackal to catch will happily eat it. Jackals are pretty protective parents. Sometimes last years youngsters stay on to help raise this years cubs. If this happens then the chances of success will be higher for the parents.

Two dogs go by the name of fox in Namibia. The cape fox and the bat-eared fox. The cape fox looks like, and is, a true fox. It is similar to foxes found in Europe and America. The bat-eared fox is the star turn. These guys look great, they have massive ears and fluffed up fur that makes them look like a brown fluffy ball. They tend to occur in family groups. You can see them round Namibia, but the Kalahari desert west of Mariental (in the mid south) seems to be a hot spot for seeing them. By the time the sun is fully up they will have disappeared, but in the early morning you can surprise family after family while driving over the gorgeous red remnant dunes of the Kalahari.

Bat-eared Foxes should be classified as insectivores rather than carnivores. They like termites, beetles and other insects plus the occasional fruit. Their thick fluffy fur is believed to provide protection when raiding termites nests. Bat-eared fox fur is used commercially and is called Macloutsie. They have more cusped teeth (over forty five) than any other non marsupial mammal. These teeth are great from crunching up the shells of insects and have jaw muscles that allow them to chew very fast. Their jaw can go up and down five times a second - all in all a real insect crunching machine.

In the wet season they can just collect insects from the surface, but in the dry season they use their big radar ears to find insects like dung beetle larvae that may be up to 30 cm underground. They then use their longs claws to dig them out. The long claws are on the front feet and if compared to other dog footprints the claw marks at the top of the print look a long way in front of the other parts of the paw. Jackals living in sandy areas may also have relatively long claws, but their footprints are much bigger than a bat-eared fox's. In winter the Kalahari can be quiet cold at night driving insects along way down so the bat-eared foxes tend to hunt more in the warmer daylight hours. Where conditions for termites are good (rainfall, soil etc), bat-eared foxes have been recorded at some of the highest densities of any dog - just under 30 foxes per square kilometer. Unlike the jackals and cape fox, bat-eared foxes do not regurgitate food for their cubs. Just imagine trying to regurgitate crushed termites! Instead the cubs mainly grow up on milk and the occasional lizard.

Wild dogs, also called cape hunting dogs, occur in Namibia but are extremely rare. The Caprivi Parks have packs that cross over from Botswana. An unsuccessful attempt was made to reintroduce them into Etosha. One difference between hunting dogs and normal domestic dogs is that hunting dogs have four rather than five toes on their front feet. For a large predator they seem to have a remarkably short lifespan amounting to around six years. Whether this is normal or the result of disease and inbreeding is not clear, but what is known is that they are one of the most endangered predators in Africa.

Plans are under way to try further reintroductions. At Harnas (north of Gobabis) they have a couple of large packs of wild dogs in big enclosures. The daily feeding trip allows you to see how fast they can rip apart a goat carcass. To successfully reintroduce wild dogs it is reckoned that you need large packs of around 40 animals. Normally just the dominant pair breed, this means that in an ideal world you would want lots of little packs to speed up the captive breeding. Wild dogs can be highly aggressive to rival packs. If you try to combine two small packs to make a larger pack suitable for reintroduction then a number of dogs will get killed in the fighting. This means you have to work with large stable packs that breed slowly. Conserving wild dogs is a long term project.

Aardwolf

You are pretty unlikely to see an aardwolf. The few places that offer nocturnal game drives may be able to find you one e.g. Hobatare and Roy's Camp. In terms of getting a photograph of one you are best off visiting the Tsaobis-Leopard Nature Park south of Karibib which have captive aardwolf and have managed to breed them. Aardwolf are related to hyena but tend to be sheep in wolf's clothing. They have a big hairy mane which they can erect to increase their apparent size, and give off a deep growl that does not match what is really a rather small animal. It is estimated that an aardwolf can make itself look 75% bigger by erecting all its hair, for people that would be equivalent to meeting the Incredible Hulk. One of the differences between hyenas and aardwolfs is that the hyena has four toes on its front feet, the aardwolf has five.

Just as hyenas have developed a stomach capable of handling just about any biological material (rotten flesh, bone etc) so aardwolfs have developed a super powerful digestive system capable of handling tough harvester termites and all the poisons they can produce. These termites are some of the few nocturnal termites, hence the aardwolf is nocturnal. They tend to avoid cold weather so winter life can be tough for the aardwolf since food is scarce on the surface and unlike the aardvark, the aardwolf lacks any real digging ability. During this time your chances of seeing an aardwolf in the early morning or late evening light are better since they are seeking alternative, less nocturnal termites to feed on.

Where the aardvark has a long tongue for extracting wood eating termites from holes, the aardwolf uses a wide tongue for licking grass eating termites off the surface. When the conditions are good an aardwolf can eat 250,000 termites in a night (over a kilogram). It all seems rather a lot of effort, and a lot of sand gets consumed by licking termites off the ground. This is evident in aardwolf droppings that have a high soil and sand content along with lots of bits of termite. The droppings are comparatively large which I guess is a reflection of their diet mainly being non digestible material. The aardwolf's use latrines (like the hyena), and finding these is often the best evidence that aardwolf's are resident in an area.

Aardwolf's have pretty big ears, and they use these to help find the harvester termites. They can hear the noise of the termites cutting up grass. This noise can be heard by people if they listen carefully.

Roan and Sable Antelope

Roan and sable have a natural grouping in Namibia since they occur in the same places, have both been subject to similar management, and are closely related. They occur naturally in the top right corner of Namibia around the Caprivi and down a bit into the main body of Namibia bordering Botswana (e.g. Khaudum park region). Back in the 1970's none of the reserves that are now in these areas existed and the authorities decided to try an ambitious relocation program. Using sedation they moved over seventy roan by Hercules airplane to western Etosha. At the time the sedating of animals for a long period during transportation was a novel technique. The technique worked well and the roan underwent quarantine. A few were released into western Etosha and the rest were moved to the Waterberg Plateau Park. A few years later the same operation was repeated for some sable antelopes. The Etosha reintroductions were not a great success so do not expect to see roan or sable in Etosha.

Sable are the aristocrats of the game farming industry. At the time of writing it costs about 100,000 Namibian dollars to buy a sable and hunters pay around 80,000 to hunt one. As they breed more, so more farms will get them and the price will come down. The magnificent horns make them popular for trophy hunters. Horns are commonly over a meter in length.

Roan have smaller horns. They are less common on game farms. I am not sure why this is, since they are one of the biggest antelope and would seem to be challenging to hunt (to me at least).

Both sable and roan need to stay reasonably close to water, and are grazers. Roan go for slightly more open and longer grass than sable. This means they are unlikely to spread widely in Namibia even with assistance. They don't move much e.g. 1-2 km a day.

Sable and roan have similar social lives. The males setup territories which are aggressively defended. The females and young form separate herds with a dominant female in charge. The dominant female decides where to take the herd while the local males try to keep the herd in their territory, especially when the females are in heat. Like many antelopes males will use their legs to prod and push females to stand up. Once up, the male tastes the female's urine to see how receptive to mating she is.

Small Antelopes

A small antelope bounds away from the roadside. How do you tell your duiker from your steenbok? Local lore will tell you that the duiker holds a guilty secret, so he bounds away without stopping to look back. The steenbok on the other hand is innocent and will bound away a few steps before pausing to look back. This rule is generally true. Duikers are also darker and rougher in colour, compared with the lighter, shinier, smooth fur of the steenbok. My favorite method is that when looking at a steenbok you can't help thinking what big ears they have (similar to a kudu). Also I have never seen a pair of duikers together, but steenbok seem perpetually to be in love and stay close to each other.

Steenbok have a curious habit of burying their droppings. You will see some turned over soil with some scrape marks on top where the steenbok has scrapped a hole, deposited its droppings and then covered them with soil - it looks more like a rabbit latrine than that of an antelope. The explanation is that the steenboks are trying to hide their presence from predators by covering up the smell. Given scent is such an important way for antelopes to communicate with each other, and that other vulnerable species of antelope don't do this, I have yet to be convinced this is a proven theory.

Baby duikers in trouble call loudly to their parents who will come running. Some hunters have learnt to imitate this call to attract the parents for "supper". Female duikers lack horns but are bigger than the males to make up for it. However they do have the thin crest of hair that looks a small horn coming out of the top centre of their head - candidates for the African pygmy unicorn.

Klipspringer habitat is hyrax habitat and both of them suffer similar predators like eagles and cats. Klipspringers can be seen in rocky places like the Namib and around the Erongo mountains. They are hyper alert since the pair take turns eating and watching. They often duet when calling, particularly after running away from something. The male calls first and the female then follows.

Klipspringers have a curious fur. It has hollow shafts that help provide insulation, it is fairly brittle, it stands erect resulting in them looking bigger than they are, and it is noisy when touched. Some people have told the story that the fur is like this to cushion the blow when klipspringers fall off rocks. More likely is that the fur helps them handle extremes of temperature, since elsewhere they can be found close to the snow line on Africa's highest mountains. Because of its tough, bouncy properties klipspringer fur was used in the past as a stuffing for riding saddles.

Dik-dik are the smallest of the antelopes in Namibia. If you want to see them visit the De le Bat camp in the Waterberg Park. Here they happily wander around the camp providing excellent photo opportunities. Dik-dik tend to be very habitat specific. The Namibian race is confined to regions with hard surfaces. They lack the foot glands that their relatives elsewhere in Africa have. Like duikers, dik-dik also have a tuft of hair on their head. Theirs is more tufty than spiky, and goes up and down according to their mood.

Dik-dik like to deposit their dropping on smelly items in their territory. You may come across dik-dik droppings that have been placed on top of elephant droppings, like a smaller pebble on a larger stone. As mentioned, steenbok go for an opposite approach, they like to bury or cover their droppings. Klipspringers favor a flat space about a meter across for their latrines. Twigs and branches next to the latrine will often have black sticky deposits on them from the klipspringer's face glands. Duikers just deposit their droppings anywhere, but this can often result in a build up at favored locations so that it looks a bit like a latrine.

The end of the Caprivi has one other small antelope, the oribi. This is sort of a cross between a duiker and steenbok. It fur is not quite so rough and dark as a duiker, neither is it as smooth and glossy as a steenbok. When running away it has a black tip to the tail. Oribi can be seen in places like the Golden Triangle.

Rodents

The biggest rodent in Namibia is the porcupine. These are reasonably common, difficult to see, but often easier to hear down a large hole. A couple of lodges (Okonjima) put out food for them, but porcupines can be very shy and often seem to turn up just after you have gone to bed. Their quills are used for all sorts of arty effects in craft shops e.g. lamp shades. They need the quills for defense because porcupine meat is very popular with both people and other carnivores. The meat has a high fat content and many a lion has tried to dine on porcupine.

Striped mice are commonly seen sprinting out of one bush to get to another just in front of your feet. These are rather attractive mice with long vertical stripes running the length of their body. They have a slightly gerbil like quality to them.

You can find rats clambering around above you in the trees around camp sites in the Namib Desert e.g. Sesserim.

Rhinoceros

White rhino were extinct in Namibia for nearly a century before they got reintroduced in the mid 1970's from the growing South African population. Twelve were moved to the Waterberg Plateau Park where they have since bred. They also occur in Etosha and a number of the game lodges round Namibia have groups of them.

If you buy a copy of South African farming magazines you will come across adverts offering white rhinos for sale as part of the growing game farming industry (about quarter of a million rand for one rhino). One of the coolest car stickers I have seen in Namibia is the sticker for the African Rhino Owners Association.

Black rhino managed to hold on in Namibia through the heavy years of poaching. In particular Etosha was a safe haven and now has a population in hundreds. In Etosha and the Waterberg Plateau Park you can compare black rhino with their cousins if you are lucky enough to see both. You never see black rhino's advertised for sale though. A few black rhino also live in a small reserve at Hardap Dam where it is possible to walk, nervously, in the same bush that they inhabit. If you are a purist you will head for Damaraland and Kaokoland in the top left corner of the country. Here is one of the last (the last?) free ranging population of black rhinos in Africa that are not restricted to a park or reserve. The remote and extreme nature of the landscape made poaching here difficult. You can join the Save The Rhino teams with their camels as they monitor the local population.

Black rhino scatter their dung with their feet - presumably to mark territory and announce their presence. The Himba tribe will tell you that it is the bad tempered natures of these beasts that makes them kick it apart.

During the poaching years Namibia undertook dehorning operations to try and make its rhino less attractive to poachers. This work received good funding from abroad. A pair of scientists studying the rhinos at the time found that mothers who had been dehorned seemed less able to defend their calves from predators like lions, and so had less success producing the next generation. The findings were controversial, an example of the conflicts to be found in nature conservation about how best to save a species.

If you want to see black rhino then the waterhole at Okaukujeo in Etosha is the place to visit. Once darkness falls the rhinos come out of the bush to drink under the spotlights. You can easily see eight at the waterhole together. Together is maybe to strong a word. They all stand around the hole and manage to both ignore, and make contact with each other at the same time. You will also see mothers with calves. Curiously black rhino calves walk beside or behind their mothers, but white rhino calves walk in front of their mothers!

In the past black rhinos have been recorded at very high densities e.g. 20 animals in an area of two and a half square kilometers. Given the size of the animals this is an impressive concentration of rhino.

Currently the black rhino population in Etosha face a problem. The park is not able to support all the waterholes it used to so the rhino have to walk further and further to find water. This need to spend more time traveling is impacting on the numbers of rhino and the population will probably decrease to match the available water supply.

Hyena

There are estimated to be around 400 spotted hyenas in Etosha. A group being studied there had a territory of around 160 km2 in the dry season when game was plentiful around the waterholes. In the wet season when the game density reduces considerably (since the animals can get water anywhere) the hyena's group territory doubled in size to compensate. The clans (groups to you and me) in the east of the park have more members than the clans in the middle of the park. By looking at the pattern of spots on an Etosha hyena researchers can tell which part of the park the hyena comes from.

The Etosha hyenas often use the drainage tunnels under the parks roads as dens for their cubs. This means you may not see them, but might have driven over them. They are also fond of having a swim and a bath so waterholes can be a good place to find them. Like the Etosha lions, some hyenas can cause problems for farmers.

Compared to other hyenas in Africa the Etosha clans seem unable to get a big enough group together to chase lions away from kills. In fact most of the time if lions find hyenas with a kill, the lions will successfully chase off the hyenas. In places like the Tanzania's Nogorogoro Crater the hyenas live in larger groups that occupy much smaller territories. This means they can not only defend their kills from lions, but on occasion steal kills made by lions.

Lions are a major cause of spotted hyena deaths, both to youngsters and elderly adults. In some studies around half the hyenas that died, did so from lions. There are other risks to hyenas; young spotted hyenas are very playful and seem to enjoy games such as who can annoy the black rhino most.

Spotted hyenas have a social organisation dominated by females. The lowliest female is still higher in the pecking order than the highest male. The females have very high levels of testosterone, often higher than in males. This seems to help in the development of the female's famous false penis. The false penises are easily visible so if you see a penis don't assume you are looking at a female. Displaying a semi erect penis is a sign of submission rather than aggression (unlike in primates!).

For many females there is a price to pay for having developed these 'masculine' genitals. When giving birth for the first time often there is not enough room for the cubs to get out. Records suggest 10% of all females die the first time they give birth. If they survive then further births are less hazardous since the damage from the first birth is permanent and makes the subsequent births easier.

Unlike dogs, hyenas do not carry food by eating it and then regurgitate it for the youngsters when they get home. Instead they carry the meat all the way home in their mouths. Understandably then hyenas tend to suckle more than bring food back.

Brown hyenas will suckle other peoples youngsters at the den but spotted hyena will only suckle their own young. This could be because brown hyena must leave the den for a few days at a time to find enough food. The cubs could not survive in the den this long without milk, so an auntie system is essential.

Hyenas do regurgitate the hair and hoof they have eaten, but things like bone get digested within a few hours inside their stomach. Teeth take a little longer, but also get consumed. The spotted hyena can bite through rhino and elephant skin, as well as crack open their massive bones. They will try biting most things. Recently a spotted hyena took to biting bits of campers sleeping outside at Sesserim.

A fun estimated fact is that a brown hyena will encounter a scent mark within 250 meters when entering another brown hyena group's territory. Brown hyenas scent mark excessively. The social life of the brown hyena seems a bit of a contradiction. These are fundamentally solitary animals that often forage alone. Where as you might see a number of spotted hyenas at a kill, you are never likely to see more than three brown hyenas eating together. So spotted hyenas are clearly more of a group animal, yet the very sparseness of the food supply and great distances that brown hyenas need to cover to find food, mean they are under pressure to form social groups for raising young and protecting territory.

Brown hyena's have long been recorded as scavenging along the Namibian coastline. The Cape Cross seal colony was considered an easy place to visit that had brown hyena. They have decreased in areas like this. One possible reason is the increase in night time fishing by anglers along the coast. This may scare the hyenas away from the shore.

Hyrax

Also known as dassies you will find them anywhere there are rocks to sunbathe on and crevices to hide in from eagles. The black eagle is so dependant of hyrax that its range is closely linked to the rocky areas where hyrax live. Hyraxes are famous for being the elephant's closest relative having features like miniature tusks and similar feet structure. This relationship with elephants is a point of discussion amongst taxonomic authorities i.e. they are not totally sure about it.

Over time the urine from hyrax colonies can create big white streaks down the rocks where they live. These tend to occur at any height as hyrax are quite happy with small or large rock faces. Given their small size (about the size of a rabbit) they have an amazing gestation period of 7 months. The young come out very well developed and are able to eat plants after four days. No months of breast feeding for hyrax.

Hyraxes tend to have short bouts of feeding where they consume large amounts of vegetation, and then spend long periods resting and digesting that may last for days. They spend a lot of time regulating their body temperature by moving around the rock face, into sunshine to warm up, and into crevices to avoid extremes of temperature.

They have a sort of barking whistle for a call that once learnt you will hear up whenever you go walking near rocks. In Windhoek they can be found in the town centre. Places like the Botanical Gardens are popular with hyrax and people often have to protect their garden plants from attack by hyraxes.

Seals

An hour and a half north of Swakopmund is Cape Cross. It was here that the Portuguese explorers first landed. Its other claim to fame is as the home to tens of thousand of fur seals. They are present all year round, but most of the young are born towards the end of the year. The site of thousands of seals sleeping, fighting and playing in the waves is impressive.

Take warm clothes because the wind and fog can make the place seem bitterly cold compared to elsewhere in Namibia. The smell from the colony is also impressive and can stay stuck to your clothes for some time afterwards. I know some local people who no longer visit the colony, just because the smell is too much.

The fur seals are culled most years and you can get seal leather goods from shops in Swakopmund.

The stylish Cape Cross Lodge next door to the colony is well worth a visit, and they do lunches and serve drinks, as well as provide accommodation.

Pangolin

Only the cape pangolin (Manis temminckii) occurs in Namibia. It occurs in most parts, but is difficult to see - or put another way you are really lucky if you see one. Personally I think pangolins are just wonderful. Partly because I have never seen one. But also because anything that is armor-plated and rumbles slowly through the bush has an attractive personality.

The young pangolin hitches a lift by holding onto his (or her) mother's tail for the first few months of life. Curiously African pangolins normally have a single offspring, but their Asian cousins have been recorded having twins and even triplets. Note; human twins are more common in Africa than Asia.

Given their diet of ants and termites pangolins no longer have teeth. Like the south american anteater their mouth is just a long toothless tube. The cape pangolin prefers ants to termites, and then only certain types of ants. You are more likely to see a pangolin in the wet season when they become less nocturnal due to changes in the depth that the ants live at.

To collect the ants pangolins have some of the longest tongues in nature. Their tongues are roughly the length of their body! When not licking up ants and termites the tongue is stored in a special pouch. The tongue links back to the bottom of the ribs allowing it to be stuck out a long way and then sucked back in quickly. Licking up ants takes a lot of saliva and the poor old cape pangolin lives in the most arid habitat of any pangolin species.

Pangolins use their scales for defense - but not just in the way you might imagine. When defending themselves they lash out with their tail. The ends of the scales create a sharp serrated edge similar to a saw that can easily draw blood. Rumor has it the pangolins scales can hold back a .303 bullet. I am unclear from what range, and who would be terrible enough to try this experiment. If all else fails and the pangolin is eaten then the scales can tear away inside the predators stomach, causing pain and on occasion death.

Cape pangolin often walk on their two hind legs. This is reflected in their body. Their tail is shorter than other species and has more weight to help provide a counterbalance. The overall appearance may seem more like a wallaby.

Zebra

Namibia has two sorts of zebra. The plains zebra Equus burchelli (also called burchell's zebra), and the mountain zebra Equus zebra hartmannae (also called the hartmann zebra). The plains zebra occurs in the plains along the top of the country, and the mountain zebra in the hilly bits from the north down to the south going along the western side of Namibia. However game farming means you could meet either species anywhere. But in the parks it will probably be plains zebra at Etosha and mountain zebra around the Namib-Naukluft and in Daan Viljoen. There are some mountain zebra in the closed western half of Etosha.

I like to think of mountain zebra as having been gone over with a fine tooth comb - hence the denser nature of their stripes. The plains zebra (being plain) doesn't worry so much about his appearance, so is less finely striped, and often has shadow stripes where he has not washed.

Why stripes? Well questions like this are similar to how long is a piece of string. There are various theories. A lionesses attacking a group of zebras may find the stripes moving in front of her eye very confusing, and so fail to catch anything. You would think that having stripes makes them pretty easy to spot so the increased visibility would cancel out this protection. Of course the way we see zebras is not the way predators like lions see them. Some people claim the stripes do in fact help camouflage zebras since they break up the outline of the zebra's body against a background of trees and similar vegetation.

A favored theory from people more expert than myself is that the stripes are a visual bonding device. Well spaced black and white patterns generate a big signal in the eyes of mammals. People often give their babies black and white mobiles above their beds, believing the increased visual stimulation will help develop their brains. For zebras the theory goes that the stripes make them want to stick together, a sort of visual magnetism. The need for this extra magnetism in zebras is because they are a pretty irritable bunch. If you see zebras fighting, it is just as likely to be females working out their position in the herd, as males protecting their herd from wandering eyes. Some people believe this constant aggression is what limits zebra herd membership to numbers in single figures e.g. 4 to 8 animals. When you see the big herds in places like Etosha they are really just lots of little herds.

This aggression means that any affection (shown by nibbling necks and legs) is normally between mothers and foals. Beyond this zebras have ritualized gestures that are similar, but do not involve them actually touching each other. A bit like two people meeting and kissing the air either side of their faces rather than the actual cheeks - it preserves their personal space, whilst making some gesture of friendship.

The visual stimuli theme continues with the mountain zebra. One of the distinguishing identification marks on their body is the 'Grid-iron' pattern at the end of their rump where the tail starts. When one mountain zebra meets another this small patch of horizontal marks is often where the zebra will place his chin – as if attracted to it.

The stripes for communication theory has other aspects to it. Mountain zebra have bigger stripes on their rumps than plains zebra. The theory suggests that due to the habitat they live in, mountain zebras have to communicate over longer distances. Longer distance means you need bigger stripes to communicate the same message that plains zebras can do over shorter distances with their narrower stripes.

So if we go for this theory that zebra herds are made up of aggressive animals held together by the strong visual attraction of stripes, can anyone explain why only zebra are attracted to the stripes. The attraction must apply to other mammals, since they have similar visual systems? When you see mixed herds of zebra and antelope is it for mutual protection, or maybe it is just because the antelopes can't drag themselves away from the zebra.

As a follow up note to the stripes - researchers have noted that on cold mornings mountain zebra stand side on to the sun, but on warmer mornings they stand head on to the sun. Apart from the difference in body area for the sunlight to warm up, there is also a large difference in the ratio of light to dark skin on the front versus the side. Side on, the dark patches are 3 times more common than the white patches. When viewed head on, the ratio is the reverse i.e. not only do they have more space to catch the sun when side on, but they have proportionally more black which is better at absorbing heat. As always with things like this you wonder coincidence or design.

Birds

Endemic Birds

Namibia has fourteen species of birds that are pretty well only found in Namibia. They occur in the coastal and inland coastal strips of the country. The birds are

Hartlaub's francolin – best looked for in the short time between first light and dawn. Listen out for the birds calls to help find them.

Ruppell's korhaan - used to be classified as a subspecies of karoo korhaan, and may interbreed with them.

Damara tern - nests up to 2 km inland from the sea. Best seen at the Walvis Bay sea front

Ruppell's parrot - see them at Waterberg plateau, or Okapuka.

Violet woodhoopoe - a noisy group of clowns moving from tree to tree.

Monterio's hornbill - at Waterberg this bird is at the bottom of the cliffs, its cousin the bradfield's hornbill lives on the rocky bits. Easy to see at Daan Viljoen Reserve.

Dune lark - Namibia's only true 100% endemic.

Barlow's lark – in 1996 it was converted from a subspecies of dune lark to become a full species. Try the main road east of Luderitz.

Gray's lark – bring a jumper when searching – they only display just before dawn and in the twilight.

Carp's Tit - Got the full species status in 1980, but in the eastern parts of its range is still easy to confuse with its relative the southern black tit.

Barecheeked babbler - could be confused with pied babbler, families work together rearing the young.

Herero Chat - is it a robin, a chat or a flycatcher, try the Spitzkoppe and Brandburg to see them.

Rockrunner - look for someone creeping round the rocky bit's of Avis Dam in Windhoek or near by at Daan Viljoen Reserve.

Whitetailed Shrike - don't mistake him for a batis, how many other ground dwelling shrikes do you know.

Bustards

Bustards are one of the groups of birds Namibia is good for. Eight species can be found in the country and they are fairly easy to see. At the big end is the kori bustard. This is the heaviest flying bird in the world. At times in Etosha you might also think them the commonest bird in the world. Their great size makes them easy to see, but also they are one of those animals that after seeing one you find another, and another, until you realise you are surrounded by them. Surveys have reckoned one kori bustard for every 16.7 km of road driven in Etosha. Like all averages this means there are places with much higher counts like the plains, and places with lower counts like the bushy woodland.

All bustards look slightly mad and irritable. It is the way their eye and beak are put together. I have always been convinced an attack is possible at any moment. In dreamy moments I suspect their name is derived from what people call them after such an attack. Ludwig's bustard was so named after a vicious attack on Ludwig.

Ruppell's korhaan is pretty well endemic to Namibia, so people want to find it. Try the gravels plains round Brandberg and Spitzkoppe, and keep yours eyes open while traveling from Usakos down to Swakopmund. Their flight tends to be slightly erratic compared to other bustards.

Bustards do great displays. The kori will wonder around all puffed up, but the korhaans seem more impressive. The Redcrested korhaan will start with a fast run and then take off going straight up into the air, then dropping down like a fluffy stone back to the ground. As you drive round these large fluffy items keep appearing to be thrown out of the long grass up into the air by invisible hands.

Weaver Birds

Famous for building great and intricate nests, there are three common species to watch out for – or at least to watch out for their nests. In terms of people seeing them, the commonest is the white-browed sparrow weaver. These chunky guys build untidy bundles of straw for a nest. The nests are normally close together in the same acacia tree. The nests look like small hairy footballs and have entrance holes facing the ground. The nests are often on the eastern side of the tree so they catch the first rays of light to warm up in mornings.

The greatest nests have to be those of the sociable weaver. These are particularly numerous in the Kalahari. The nests are massive and sit in larger trees. They support colonies numbering hundreds of sociable weavers. They look like a thatched roof, similar to the thatched roofs beloved of game lodges and poolside bars round Namibia. The birds keep building these nests year on year until the sheer weight breaks the branch they are balanced on. You often find trees with a large broken branch on the ground which is still partially covered by the old nest. Above it a new nest is slowly expanding until it will break the next branch.

These nests are so large that they become focal points for other species. Pygmy falcons like to nest in them. Look for a large hole in the social weaver nest with a white ring round it indicating the pygmy falcon nest. Other species like to use the social weaver nest as a base upon which to build their own nests.

This permanent nest life style has a number of advantages when you live in the desert. The nests provide very good insulation against the extremes of weather outside; they are warm in winter and cool in summer. It also means that when rains do appear the social weavers already have a nest and are ready to take advantage of the food produced by the rainfall. Within six days of it raining they can produce eggs, and given suitable conditions they can manage up to four broods in a season.

The one confusing thing about social weaver nests (at least to me) is how come a bird that builds such massive nests, and in places like the Kalahari has so many nests, seems comparatively difficult to see. I would expect them to be everywhere, but somehow after leaving the nest they just disappear into the surrounding area.

The southern masked weaver makes up the trio, though his less common but close relative the lesser masked weaver should also be included with him. Look at the colour of the eye ring to tell them apart. These guys build the more traditional weaver bird nest. That is they start by twisting bits of grass or palm leaf round a branch to form a loop. Using this frame they weave a circular ball on to the end of the branch. The male normally makes a couple of these. I assume because females like a choice, but it may also be because the nests often seem to get blown off the branch by strong winds.

Terns and Skimmers

Head down to the coast of Namibia and you will probably come across signs warning you about nesting damara terns. These little terns have a good publicity team helping to protect them. They are not quite as rare as once thought, however in places the popular hobby of off road driving makes breeding difficult for the terns. A great place to watch them is the lagoon at Walvis Bay. You can see a good selection of terns here. The massive caspian terns (orange bill), the not quite so big swift terns (yellow bill), then the sandwich terns (black bill with yellow tip). Next comes a range of medium terns like the arctic and common. Finally we find the little and damara tern. Once you get your eye in the damara are easy to spot. Their tails just look really short - and are grey on the adults. They have a full black cap and give a distinctive chic-chic call. It is a slightly subtle call similar to two small stones being clicked together.

Ringing has shown Common Terns in Namibia migrate as far as Finland and back.

However elegant terns are skimmers beat them. They have big long wings, dark on top and light underneath. They are very smart and attractive, but when roosting have the appearance of clowns waiting to join the air force. On rivers like the Zambezi and Okavango (e.g. Mahango park) you will see them going about their business as the sun goes down. In my mind this is one of the definitive sights of African rivers. As the waters go down and sandbanks appear they collect on little sandy islands where you can get good views of their amazing bills.

Oxpeckers

Namibia has both of the world's two species of oxpecker; the yellowbilled and redbilled oxpecker. The names tells you how to tell them apart (the yellowbilled has some red on it's bill, but the redbilled has no yellow at all). They occur mainly in the Caprivi Parks e.g. Mahango, but also along the Angolan border. They need large mammals to sit on and collect parasites off, so this mainly restricts them to the parks and reserves. The use of cattle dips has driven them off most farmland.

They have slightly different feeding methods. The redbilled has more of a scissor technique, the yellowbilled is more of a plucker. I guess this is a slight form of niche since it must be easier to pluck from inside an ear? They do not just eat the fleas and ticks found on their hosts skin. They also enjoy an open wound, even if it was caused by them pulling of some blood sucking tick. Indeed they get the tick, then feed off the bloody wound, and finally feed off the maggots that infect the wound. Makes you wonder if the oxpecker should be called a parasite.

Oxpeckers seem to have preferences for their hosts. A study elsewhere in Africa found a pecking order (pun intended) with giraffe and cape buffalo being the favorites. I have not seen them at night but apparently the yellowbilled oxpeckers like to spend the night roosting on their mammal hosts (for warmth?), whilst the redbilled prefer trees or reed beds.

Bee-Eaters and Rollers

The great thing about this group is that they are pretty big, very colourful, and like to sit on top of objects so they can be seen by people. Around Windhoek the swallow tailed bee-eater is the commonest bee-eater. They like to make short sweeping flights out from a perch, and you can see the forked tail that gives them their name. In the summer european bee-eaters turn up to appear in groups like little fighter squadrons.

If you travel up north then your choice of bee-eaters improves. In particular the north east Caprivi has colonies of carmine bee-eater. The brilliance of these birds can not be overstated. Some of the lodges like Kalizo on the Zambezi can take you on a boat into the middle of such a colony to be surrounded by pink and red flashing birds. If you want to do this make sure you time your trip right because they all disappear in the winter (March to October) and you may be lucky to see even a single bird.

Compared to bee-eaters, rollers are much more of a chunky, thick set bird. At times the lilac breasted roller seems to occupy every second telegraph pole as you drive from Windhoek to Etosha (chanting goshawks being on the other posts). Given a fire sizable numbers of these birds will collect along with hornbills to feed off the insects and other life the fire flushes out. On such occasions you can drive through a flurry of blue and lilac colour praying you don't hit too many.

The oddball of this collection is the purple roller. Unlike his relatives this is a slightly muddy coloured bird. The plumage colour alone will not convince you it is a roller. They also tend to sit inside bushes more often than on top of them. Despite all these anti roller characteristics his chunky body shape helps give away his roller origins.

Eagles

Namibia has a good selection of eagles. The fish eagle is more widespread than you might first guess, though it is generally confined to places with water. This can be a small waterhole where animals other than fish become part of the diet e.g. terrapins, flamingos, hyrax, carrion. When the fishing is good they seem to have a rather easy life. One study estimated fish eagles only spend an average of 8 minutes hunting each day.

How can you tell the male fish eagle from the near identical female? Well if your eyes can judge it well enough he is a little smaller (as is the way with all male eagles). Alternatively you can use your ears - the male has a higher pitched call, and when calling as a pair the female tends to call first.

Fish eagles are a species that recently showed the impact of humans on wildlife populations in Namibia. During the conflict on the Angolan border most people left an area along the Kavango river. A couple of intrepid bird watchers carried on their regular wetland bird counts and produced a data set that gives some indication of the impact of people on the local ecosystem. Before the war fish eagles were not present. The average number of wetland birds was around 320 for every 10 km of river. With the arrival of fighting people left the area. The fish eagles promptly returned with an average of 3 birds per 10 km of river, and the total wetland bird count increased to an average of 940 birds per 10 k, stretch of river. The overall bird species richness for the area also increased once war broke out. Similar improvements in the fish population also took place. This helps to give some idea of the pressure humans place on their environment.

A lot of eagles come and go according to the season i.e. migrate. Sometimes the same species can divide up into different populations. For example the booted eagle has both a resident population, and one that migrates in and out of Namibia.

Each year steppe eagles come all the way from places like Russia at the top of the world, down to Namibia at the bottom. They arrive in time for the rains so they can feast! What brings such a mighty predator all this way? Termites. I can not help thinking this is a damming statement about winter life in Russia. An individual eagle can eat over 2000 termites a day. Large flocks of eagles collect together after the rains to feast on the emerging termites. They are joined by other migrants like storks who also enjoy a good termite.

People often confuse the black breasted snake eagle with the martial eagle. They are similar but the martial is obviously bigger and is dark under wings compared to the clear white of the snake eagle. Remember black breasted snake eagle does not mean black underneath, more like black from the breast up (as the name says).

The black and bateleur eagles are two attractive eagles that many visitors enjoy. The black is linked to mountain regions with cliffs to nest on, and hyraxes to hunt. You can find them on the rocks next to the restaurant at Daan Viljoen. The bateleur can be found in Etosha and is also seen from roadsides when driving round the country north of Windhoek. From a distance look for the very curly up ends to the bateleur's wings along with the comparatively short tail.

Ostrich

The Latin name for the ostrich is Struthio camelus. As you might guess the camelus bit comes from camels. Both camels and ostriches are desert animals, accustomed to vast open space and not a lot of water. Ostriches and camels both have long eyelashes, a case of convergent evolution for desert living. As part of their adaptation to this landscape the ostrich has developed quiet excellent eyesight and is difficult to sneak up on. However he is not the brightest bird. This is reflected in an ostrich's eye balls and brain. Both are roughly the same size.

Ostrich farming has been popular in Namibia but the country is not well suited to compete with the big South African ostrich farms. South Africa has a better environment for quickly rearing large numbers of ostriches i.e. water and pasture, rather than desert. You will find ostrich on many of the restaurant menu's and in the supermarkets, but often it will have been imported from South Africa.

The ostrich farm at Okahandja is set up for tourists and gives a nice tour letting you learn a lot. You can even sit on the back of one. Mariental is the centre of Namibia's ostrich industry. Just before entering the town on the Windhoek road you can see large enclosures (next to the new abattoir) that have hundreds of ostriches in them.

Ostrich have surprising droppings. They look remarkably like a large carnivores dropping rather than a herbivore or birds, and they are white.

Hornbills

Most people know what a hornbill is. Sometimes they confuse them with toucans, but there are no toucans in Namibia so that makes things easy. Hornbills are pretty visible, largish, and have massive beaks so people like them. Through watching Walt Disney's The Lion King children all seem to know what a hornbill is. Hornbills are good for road trips where you see them crossing the road in front of you, or sitting on trees and posts as you drive along. Try to look at the beak colour as you whiz past. Yellow billed hornbill and red billed hornbill speak for themselves. The grey hornbill has a black/grey bill with a whitish banana drawn on it. These tend to be the common hornbills you see along roads and round houses.

The popular hornbill with dedicated birdwatchers is the monterio's hornbill, because Namibia is practically the only place where they occur. Daan Viljoen is a good place to see them, and they have been studied here by zoologists. Just to make life confusing a similar looking hornbill, bradfield's hornbill occurs in Namibia. They do not overlap in range much but make sure your monterio's has some obvious white bits on his wing. The other easy clue is that monterio's occur on the plains and bradfield's like rock faces. So much so that you can see one on a tree in front of you, and the other on a cliff behind.

Hornbills are not the world greatest flyers. Zoologists at Daan Viljoen have noticed Augur Buzzards turning up each year to feed on the young hornbills learning to fly in the bushes. Zoologists have also been studying the genetic make up of hornbills in Namibia and are proposing that the red billed hornbill in Namibia should be recognized as a distinct sub-species or even species.

The Caprivi has a few extra species hornbill more suited to woodland like the trumpeter hornbill. Though extending out of the Caprivi to places like Etosha I think of my favorite hornbill as a Caprivi bird. If you have never seen a ground hornbill prepare for a shock. These are big birds. They live on the ground looking for snakes, lizards and insects. The often go around in family groups and are another bird species that seems to have personality. If you get a good view you may see their long eyelashes which are unusual in a bird.

Secretary Bird

Widespread throughout Namibia, you can see them anywhere there is a little vegetation and food to hunt (insects, snakes, rodents etc). In flight they look big and lanky with half dangling legs. Many people claim they got their name from the black feathers sticking out from behind their ear, and black "coat" that make them look like a secretary from some novel by Charles Dickens. An alternative theory is that their name comes from the Arabic "saqr-et-tair" meaning "Hunter Bird".

They are excellent martial arts demonstrators. They have lightening fast and very powerful kicks that they use to stun and kill prey like snakes.

Flamingo

Namibia is the best place in the world to see flamingos, and not a lot of people know that. The population around Walvis Bay has large numbers of lesser and greater flamingos. You can sit on the Esplanade at Walvis lagoon and have large groups of them busily feeding 10 meters from you. The simple rule I work to is that lesser's are smaller but have a greater shade of pink. The two sorts get on so well together because the greater goes for food in the surface water, and the lesser sieves the lower mud for food.

These are the same sort of flamingos that you get in East Africa at famous places like Lake Nakuru. They differ from their East African cousins in their longevity. Your Namibian flamingo will live longer than his East African equivalent Why? Well like most of nature it is all about sex. Many of the Namibian birds breed up in the salt pans of Etosha. Most years you will see some flamingos up in Etosha over the summer. However the majority remain behind at the coast because they know there is not enough water in the salt pans for them to breed. The flamingos hang around the coast until a good rainy year comes along. Somehow they can tell that the Etosha pan is full of water and they all leave the coast for Etosha to start breeding. It is reckoned they attempt breeding about every three year. To breed successfully they need good rains, this means the Namibian birds have only breed successfully five times in forty years! Thus they need to live longer so they get the chance to successfully breed. No one has explained to me how they manage this feat - is it diet, or just years of evolution, or something else. The implication being that you could have a race of people who naturally live for twice as long as the rest of the human population. Or is this just a moral story – abstain from sex and live longer.

Some of the coastal flamingos go to Botswana to breed so if you see juvenile flamingos at the coast it is not proof of breeding at Etosha.

To get the best photos of flamingos they should be flying. They are just gorgeous. If you can make it down to Sandwich Bay south of Walvis you can see flamingos flying against red sand dunes, a wonderful sight.

Starlings

Starlings are another high profile group of birds. They hang around lodges and towns making them easy to see. Round Windhoek the pale winged starlings will quite happily watch you shopping in Independence Avenue. They are easiest to identify when flying since that is when their big round pale wing spots are visible. Given their body size they also seem to have rather oversized wings.

For some reason I associate glossy starlings with water and drinking. They will happily hang nearly upside down on a dripping tap for a drink, or find a bird bath for a good splash. They are a gorgeous colour but you can not help looking at their bright yellow eyes and wondering whether you would trust them.

Compared to the glossy and pale winged starlings that go around in couples or families, wattled starlings tend to move around in larger groups. You could nearly call them pied in appearance, but they are just a bit too grey to make it. Early morning and late evening seems to send them hurrying by in groups heading to and from some secret home.

Burchell's starling is big. At the start you wonder if it is a glossy starling, but you can not remember them being that big, or having such a long tail. They often like the lawns and tree around lodges and you will see them at the Etosha lodges like Namutoni.

The final member of the starlings most people see is the plum coloured starling. This is one of those brilliant coloured smart birds. Somehow the white belly makes his purple all the brighter. Down south you tend to see individuals, but up north along the river banks you can get groups of them sitting in trees like bright purple flowers.

These are all the starlings that people see on the regular tours round Etosha, Swakopmund and Sossusvlei. The starling enthusiast will want to head up to the north east corner of Namibia where another four species of starling can be found. These guys start to make you life complicated with tail shape and shades of colour becoming more important in helping to identify them.

Pied Babbler

Pied Babblers are birds with character. They are gregarious in a way that reminds you of a mongoose pack. Most social birds are pleasant to watch, but with these guys it is more like laid on entertainment. As their name suggested they are black and white birds. The distinct white plumage seems out of place in this habitat making them very easy to see. They wander through the bush making a noise and checking everything out. They form a circle round some object of interest. Then they start to have a conversation about what it is, can you eat it, and who should try to peck it first. Groups can get up to double figures in size. Otjibamba lodge just south of Otjiwarongo always seem to have a group round the lodge somewhere.

Sunbirds

Namibia has the right number of sunbirds for a country. Not like parts of East Africa where there are too many species and it can get confusing, but more than one species so as to keep it interesting. The other advantage is that they are relatively easy to tell apart, plus easy to see. The scarletchested and dusky sunbirds are common in Windhoek gardens. The male scarletchested is one of those stunning at 30 meters birds and at the right angle just catches your eye like a shining light. At first so overwhelmed was I by the scarletchested sunbirds that I just assumed the dusky sunbirds were female scarletchested sunbirds. Having overcome my blindness I can now recognize dusky sunbirds and appreciate the impressive song that such a small bird can produce.

Sunbirds are pretty well adapted to desert life. Out in the Namib and similar dry places you will find dusky sunbirds pretty common. This always seems surprising given the cold nights and lack of flowers most of the year, but they have a more general diet than you might suspect.

Don't be fooled by the colours of the Sunbirds in the bird books. Their plumage varies considerably depending on how the light is hitting them. Many a green or purple feather can appear black.

For some reason people in Namibia do not put out bird feeders for sunbirds in the way they do for hummingbirds in America. You can see special sunbirds food and feeders advertised on the Internet, but they do not seem to have caught on even though people put out bird seed to attract finches and weavers.

Mousebirds

I equate mousebirds with 4 year old boys. They go around in little groups, they are terribly sweet to watch, they have yet to fully master the art of movement, they investigate anything, there are always more around you than you first see, and they are highly destructive.

Mousebirds are great to watch as they clamber around the bushes. They are common in town gardens. Their natural curiosity means they seem to have a far better idea of the fruit in your garden than you do. Paw-Paw, prickly pear, blossoms on a tree; they all get ripped apart by gangs of these raiders who descend on gardens.

Mousebirds superficially seem to be related to the hoatzin from South America. Both are awkward flyers who seem just as awkward climbers, or rather clamberers in tree. Apart from this inability to fly and hop properly mousebirds have a few other fun features. On an early cold morning you can catch a mousebird sitting on a branch because it will not yet be warm enough to fly away. Also mousebirds keep their head down while drinking and suck up the water, a trick they share with doves. All other birds take water into their mouth and then lift the head up to let the water trickle down. Mousebirds are not closely related to doves so why do they both have this ability? I have no idea, but again it raises the question of how much of life is planned, and how much is coincidence.

Most birds sleep in a horizontal position, on a ledge, on a branch or on the ground. Mousebirds sleep vertically. Watch them in a bush or tree and you will see their longs legs ending up nearly next to their face, leaving their body in a vertical, verging on upside down posture, a bit like a hanging parrot.

Remember there are two species of mousebird in Namibia. So rather than just saying mousebird, try to make sure you know which species you are looking at (look at the colours on the face and back).

Seabirds

Namibia has a long coastline that mostly borders the biologically productive Bengula current. The current is an upwelling of cold water that brings lots of food (nutrients) for the marine life to feed on. The seabirds are at the top of this food chain and large numbers feed off the Namibian coastline. Studies of biodiversity have shown that warm water seas tend to have less food but many different sorts of marine life. Cold waters like the Bengula have fewer species, but the species they do have tend to be very plentiful. This is also reflected in the seabirds where you often get colonies numbering thousands of just one species.

These large gatherings have been the focus of Namibia's guano industry. Guano is no longer the white gold it once was, but it still has commercial value. Many decades ago people realised that if they could build extra island space for the seabirds to nest and rest on, then they could probably get more guano. So they built a series of wooden platforms along the coast from Walvis Bay up to Cape Cross. These have been very successful in attracting seabirds and now have significant colonies of breeding birds. The platform just north of Walvis is very easy to see. You can drive off the Swakopmund to Walvis road and get very close. Look for the pelicans and other less common seabirds amongst the endless stream of cape cormorants.

The cape, bank and crowned cormorants are all endemic to South West Africa so make sure you tick all three species off when visiting Walvis and Swakopmund. Cormorants can see well both above and below water, a difficult trick that humans can not manage. They achieve this trick by having a soft cornea that allows it to flatten when they are underwater and so compensate for the change in vision needed.

To see the "hard core" seabirds like petrels, shearwaters and albatrosses you are best off taking one of the cruises out of Walvis Bay or Long Beach that look for dolphins and seals. You have a chance of jackass penguin on such a trip. Otherwise good old fashioned sea watching with a telescope should pick up things like skuas.

Vultures

These days vultures are big business in conservation circles. Worldwide many species have declined. In Asia they have been dying in large numbers from a mysterious disease. Some species have now made it to the various worldwide lists of endangered species. Within Namibia the cape griffon vultures have been reduced to a handful of birds at Waterberg. One poisoned carcass killed 10% of the lappet-faced vultures in the massive Namib-Naukluft Park which is a major home to these impressive birds.

Vultures have massive home ranges. They can easily cover 100 km and may feed anywhere in an area covering a couple of million hectares. If just one farmer amongst a few hundred farms puts out poison there is a good chance the vultures will find it. This highlights one reason vulture populations are vulnerable. Many birds may converge on a single carcass, so one event can have a large impact.

At first glance vultures are easy to identify. You have the white-backed which have long necks, and the lappet-faced which are massive and dark with short necks. But each one of these has a cousin to add confusion. The very rare cape vultures look similar to white-backed vultures, and the white-headed vulture looks similar to a lappet-faced but has a white head. So be careful to check your vultures.

The cape vultures in Namibia are at the extreme of their range. Their nearest breeding neighbors are 1000 km away in Botswana. Currently it looks as if they have ceased to breed in Namibia and given their isolated status no longer seem a viable population. Part of the reasons for their decline may be because of habitat change. After feeding these vultures require a reasonable space for take off. They do not like thick scrub and prefer open grasslands. The area where they live at Waterberg has become more overgrown due to overgrazing so driving them further away when foraging. This has had a knock on effect of bringing them into contact with poisons on farms. Cape vultures are currently being reintroduced at Waterberg to try and rebuild this endangered population.

Compared too other parts of the world I am always amazed at how invisible vultures are in Namibia. The commonest species, the white-backed, is widespread. Yet you can go for weeks without seeing one then suddenly find thirty coming out of a bush trying to take off after filling up on a dead animal.

Sandgrouse, Pigeons and Doves

To many Europeans a game bird is something like a grouse. There are no grouse in Namibia but the closest thing to a grouse seems to be the sandgrouse. They fly fast and furious and look really attractive up close. With your eyes open you will see sandgrouse as you move round the country. They often sit next to, or on the edge of gravel roads believing they are invisible e.g. in Etosha and the Namib

To get the full impressive nature of these birds you need to be at a waterhole in the morning or evening. Hundreds to thousands come to drink. You can sit and watch as wave after wave arrives. Why do they drink in such large numbers and at set times? Some theories suggest it allows knowledge of good feeding areas to be passed between them. I just wonder if it because that it is the cooler part of the day.

To make life confusing one species of Namibian sandgrouse is called the double-banded sandgrouse. Presumably because of the double band on its breast. However the namaqua sandgrouse which lives alongside it also has a double band on its breast! When looking at a male sandgrouse look at its head markings rather than trying to work out the colour of the bands. In flight the problem is easier because the namaqua has a long pointed tail just like the namaqua dove (does namaqua really mean long pointy tail rather than refer to a region?)

Namibia has a number of pigeons and doves without long pointy tails. For attractiveness the african green pigeon must get the medal. Large, rounded and bright green it can be found sitting in the trees up north. The laughing dove is one of the ubiquitous birds that you find everywhere in the country. The namaqua dove competes for attractiveness. For some reason the campsite area at Okaukujeo in

Etosha always has a large friendly flock of these birds which elsewhere I only see in small groups or as individuals.

Hamerkop

For a 'wetland' bird hamerkops occur in a rather a lot of places including Windhoek. They create massive domed nests and will use whatever is at hand to construct them. In places close to human habitation all manner of man made objects can be used. Items as bizarre as underpants and socks have been found in the nests.

Owls

The owls in Namibia are spotted eagle owl, barn owl, marsh owl, scops owl, pearlspotted owl, giant eagle owl, whitefaced owl, barred owl. Then you get wood owl and pel's fishing owl up in Caprivi and cape eagle owl just touching the bottom of Namibia.

Pel's is the bird that most people talk about seeing. It has achieved that romantic status that puts it on most peoples wish lists, a bit like the condor in America. If you want to see pel's then you are best off using guides who can take you to the birds. Often it is best to nip across to Botswana where a number of the lodges have regular sightings. One difference between pel's and the other owls is that pel's are noisy in flight. This is because their prey, fish, live under water so there is no need to fly quietly. If you are cruising the waterways of the Caprivi at night and a big noisy owl flies out you now know what it is.

Spotted eagle owl's are widespread both in towns and country. You can see them at night in Windhoek. They call the most between May to August at the start of the nesting season.

Barn owls are also widespread. Their diet changes according to location, gerbils in the desert, mice and rats in the grassier locations. A barn owl was responsible for discovering a new species of mammal - the first grant's golden mole (which is found in the Namib Desert) was identified from a barn owl pellet!

Scoops owl are normally heard rather than seen. Find a recording before visiting the country so you know what to listen out for. The Halali camp in Etosha is a good place to see scoops. It always pays to ask people working at lodges if they know of a spot in the camp with a roosting owl. Pearlspotted owls can often be found out in the daytime. Waterholes and riverbanks tend to be good places to see owls. So if you are watching a waterhole at night keep your eyes open. You often see giant eagle owl at the floodlit Okaukujeo waterhole in Etosha.

Did you know that cats have better night vision than owls, and owls have similar hearing to humans. The trick owls have is a far better ability than people to pinpoint where a sound comes from.

Other Animals

Crocodiles

Crocodiles occur naturally in the rivers and swamps of the north. They have been heavily hunted in many areas so that the really big crocs are pretty well gone. Don't be fooled into thinking that the water is safe though. Last year thirteen people were killed by crocodiles in Namibia. Now for a country that is mostly desert and has a small population thirteen seems quite high. Across Africa crocodiles are by far the most dangerous predator for people. Local people may be a little fatalistic about it, but the attitude of tourists can seem just as bad at times. At lodges children are left to play on the sand banks of the Zambezi within view of basking crocodiles. And that is the crocodiles you can see. If you go for a walk in a park like Mahango and Mudumu you can easily find yourself pretty close to a crocodile so beware. A boat trip on the rivers and swamps at the end of the Caprivi is a good way to see them.

Crocodiles can be great travelers. They can easily travel tens of kilometers across hills and mountains. In this way they can spread to individual lakes that would seem safe from crocodiles. A big crocodile only needs to feed a few times a year, so they can easily survive in such isolated places. Many of the lodges like to keep one or two crocodiles for tourists, which means they have an extended (but extremely low density) range round the country.

Windhoek holds an annual fair. One year a gentleman from South Africa came to the fair with his crocodile. For transport he decided just to put the crocodile in the back of his pick up - this is very much a southern Africa philosophy of life i.e. anything can be transported in the back of a pick-up truck. On arriving at the show ground the crocodile was missing. At the showground that evening rumors spread claiming that the crocodile was loose in the showground under one of the beer tables. In fact the pick-up had stopped on the way up to Windhoek and the crocodile had just climbed out. He was found a few days later by an observant motorist driving through the desert who thought he saw a crocodile next to the road!

Crocodiles have remarkably good senses and ability to communicate. Their eyesight is good so you must creep up very carefully if you are trying to get close to one. The females can call their young back to safety by vibrating their bodies in the water as a form of communication. The males have various techniques from tail slapping to blowing fountains of water that they use to communicate with others. They are comparatively bright and have been known to form groups for cooperative hunting techniques like herding fish.

To see some really big crocodiles up close visit the Crocodile Ranch at Otjiwarongo. The oldest is a 90 year old male. You can learn about how stressed out young crocodiles get without their mother about, and how nile crocodiles are the only crocodiles with pigment hence their preference by the leather trade. The reason all the big adults lack pigment is that over the years it gets bleached out by the sun.

Snakes

Namibia has a good selection of snakes and they are reasonably common. That said unless you actively search for them you are probably not going to see many (or any). You need to take care when walking in the bush. Most snakes will move out of your way but the puff adder which accounts for many accidents tends to try and protect itself by hiding rather than moving. This trust in its camouflage means it regularly gets stepped on by walkers.

Puff adders have cytotoxic venom that destroys the body's cells. Other venomous snakes like mambas have neurotoxic venom that causes paralysis and so stops people being able to breathe. This takes a while (7 to 15 hours for an adult), so there is normally time to get to a hospital for treatment.

Many species of snake are multi-dimensional, in that they go down holes and up trees. If you are looking for them the branches of bushes are good places, as are holes in termite mounds. Tarmac roads are a good place to see snakes. Often they have been killed (and squashed) by a car, otherwise they cross in front of you as you drive along. Quite a number of snake species will pretend to be dead if they can not escape. This includes some of the poisonous species so if it looks dead make sure with a stick or something before going to close.

The biggest Namibian snake and the only one capable of eating a small person is the southern african python. This is fairly widespread in the northern half of Namibia but with a preference for water. Like all pythons it kills by "crushing" rather than poison. After eating a large animal they have difficulty moving so become vulnerable to attack from people and dogs. As with most snakes the female pythons are bigger than the males with a length of 5 meters being possible.

Snakes have a number of predators, secretary bird, ground hornbill, honey badger and eagles are just a few of the species who will happily take on a snake. There are also snakes that eat snakes. The cape file snake kills venomous and non venomous snakes. However when captured it does not bite, but may empty its bowels over you. Large snouted cobras will kill puff adders. Rather than "dog eat dog", "snake eat snake" may be a more appropriate saying.

One of Namibia's more famous snakes is the sidewinder. This is a mildly poisonous adder that lives in the dunes of the Namib. On sunny days it is possible to see the distinctive marks made by sidewinder snakes going across the dunes and ending at the location where they have buried themselves into the sand. Like many Namib inhabitants it obtains moisture by letting the coastal fog precipitate on its body.

If you want a closer look at some snakes there is a small snake park in Swakopmund.

Lizards

Lizard spotting and chasing is always a popular pastime, especially with children and dogs. At night they are replaced by geckos. To find a gecko try a little nocturnal walk with a torch and look behind objects near walls and above your head.

The big lizards are the monitors. These eat pretty well anything they can catch including crunchy items like baby tortoises. Namibia has two species, the rock and the water monitor. Their names tells you all you need to know about where to find them, with the rock being widespread, and the water restricted to wet places. A boat trip along a river in the Caprivi will normally find a few water monitors resting in the sun.

A Namibian speciality are barking geckos. Namibia has two endemic species. These geckos live in burrows in the desert. At night the males come out to call and make loud clicking sounds. Their burrows amplify the calls to an impressive level. They are very difficult to see even though you can hear them calling all round you. Campsites like Sesserim and the Ugab Wilderness Community campsite are good places to listen out for them.

When visiting the sand dunes at near Walvis Bay or Sossusvlei you find little shovel-nosed lizards running around the hot dune sand. These are the lizards made famous by many a Namib documentary program. Once the sand heats up they perform a sort of dance lifting opposing front and back legs to reduce the area touching the hot sand. If you can stand the heat of the sand they are entertaining to watch doing the dance and skating over the sand looking for seeds and other food that collects in the eddies from the wind over the dunes.

Scorpions

These guys are pretty common and there are a number of species. They love rocky areas and are a constant threat to all the geologists working in

Namibia. These guys pick up stones, watch out for snakes under the stones, then check the stones for scorpions before they can look at the actual rock.

A simple rule of thumb is the thinner the tail the less poisonous the scorpion. The thicker the tail, the more poisonous. The most poisonous species has a very thick tail and lives in desert regions.

As if stinging is not enough, some species of scorpion can flick their venom at you. Remember, whether flicking or stinging they can only attack what is in front of them i.e. you are safe behind a scorpion because you can not be stung (until they turn round).

If you want to find a scorpion then look under rocks and in cracks on rocky walls. Alternatively go out at night with a UV light. Scorpions fluoresce in UV light (but only after their new skins have hardened).

Spiders

Spiders are worth avoiding in Namibia. Namibia does have a highly venomous species that can even kill on occasion. Luckily they tend to be restricted to the sandy desert and rarely come into contact with people. The brown button spider does associate with humans though. This is a relative of the black window but less toxic. A bite can still hurt a lot and cause swelling in adults, let alone in children. These spiders like to hide in towels and clothing so it is a good idea to shake anything before letting it touch your skin.

Rather more obvious, and less dangerous, are the baboon spiders. So called because baboons like to eat them. These look like the spiders you see in films. They are big, walk fast and very hairy. Unlike their South American cousins these guys do not shed their hairs if touched. They have a big bite with some venom but it is more painful than poisonous. Someone performed an experiment to test the toxicity of baboon spiders. Some guinea pigs were put in with these spiders and the guinea pigs died.

The autopsy showed not that they died from the poison, rather they died from fright!

A fun group are the sun spiders. These can appear very big and often seem to have ten rather than eight legs. The final two are extended mouth parts rather than legs. They try to avoid sunlight and in doing so have created their reputation for chasing people. What happens is you turn over a stone to reveal a sun spider. His shelter gone the sun spider now tries to head for the nearest shade which is your shadow on the ground. Seeing the sun spider heading your way you immediately start to move backward. So your shadow moves, and because of this the sun spider also has to move towards you once more to get back in the shade. This carries on and hence gives the impression that the sun spider is chasing you.

Sun spiders are in fact harmless, but have a reputation for stealing hair from animal's fur, including the bushy beards of Afrikaans men out camping.

The Gladiator

In the world of insects Namibia has a recent claim to fame. A whole new order of insect was recently discovered living here. Technically referred to as Mantophasmatodea, they have also been dubbed Gladiator (they coincided with the film of the same name). The last time a new order of insect was discovered was over 80 year ago.

A museum worker in Europe started noticing animals that were different in museum collections and this led to a search for them on Namibia's Brandberg Mountain. The mountain is a sort of island in the sea of desert and is full of insects and plants that are not found in the surrounding area. After a number of nights finding nothing the climate changed and the researchers who were about to go home discovered lots of these new insects.

The new insect is a sort of stick insect crossed with a praying mantis.

Other Invertebrates

Most places will have a good collection of praying mantis and stick insects scattered amongst the trees and bushes. The stick insects can be picked up if handled very carefully.

Look in sandy ground for evidence of ant lion traps. The larvae create small (1-2 cm across) inverted volcano shape holes in the sand for unwary prey to fall into. As the prey falls in the larvae sitting at the bottom flicks grains of sand onto the sides of the hole to help the victim slide down to the bottom. Here open jaws are waiting to hold the prey while its juices are sucked out by the larvae. You can see this if you gently brush the sides of a trap with a blade of grass. You often see old holes, so look for a piece of newly raked sand to ensure the holes have a hungry resident hidden at the bottom.

You will find a lot of dung in Namibia and accompanying it a lot of dung beetles. There are many different species. The famous ones create large balls of dung which they roll away and bury with eggs inside. The exterior of the dung ball hardens to protect the eggs, and once hatched the young beetles feast on the soft interior for their first meal. Other species of dung beetle will just lay their egg beneath a pile of dung in between feeding off the dung themselves.

Tampan ticks are blood sucking insects that sit in ambush amongst the shade of large trees like acacias in arid areas. When an animal seeks shade under the tree the ticks can sense its movement and the carbon dioxide from its breathing. They emerge and start to climb on to the host. Their saliva has a chemical to deaden any feeling so they can stay feeding on the unsuspecting hosts blood. The hosts can be human just as easily as antelope. The ticks can not stand strong heat so moving back out into the open causes them to jump off and seek shelter under the shady tree once more.

It would be unfair not to mention the many marine invertebrates found along Namibia's coast. Some like the rock lobster have economic importance. They and other shellfish are available to eat in the bars and restaurants of Swakopmund, and are a Namibian export. A walk along the Walvis Bay lagoon at low tide will reveal hundreds of jellyfish stranded on the mud. The thousands of coastal flamingos rely on rich macro and microscopic life to be found in the coastal waters.

Chameleons

Keep an eye out for chameleons. These occur throughout the country. They are easiest to spot crossing roads, especially in the spring, when love encourages them to move. If you are a tourist visiting Windhoek check out the Tintinplast gardens next to the parliament for chameleons.

I am told a good way to find a chameleon is to look for them at night. They come out to the ends of branches to hunt at these times and you may see their silhouettes or catch them in your torch light. Their bodies also gently fluoresce after the light leaves them so helping you see their shape in the tree. I have to confess to so far not having luck using this method but more than one person has recommended it.

The short bushes in the desert as you approach the coast are also meant to be full of little Chameleons (e.g. road from Brandburg to Hentis Bay).

Domestic Animals

I was told a nice story by a Hereo colleague that explained the widely differing behaviors of dogs, goats and donkeys on roads in Namibia. One day a dog, a goat and a donkey were hitch-hiking to get to the next town. A car stopped and said they could all have a lift for 10 dollars each. They all said okay and got in. The donkey paid his money and sat down. The dog paid his and sat down. The goat didn't have any money so he asked the dog to lend him 10 dollars. The dog agreed and gave him the loan, and the goat settled down. As the car approached the town the goat suddenly stood up, jumped out of the window and ran away. To this day if you meet a goat on the road he will run away afraid the dog might be in the car trying to get his money back. If you meet a dog he will chase after you hoping the goat is in your car so he can catch it and get his money back. And if you meet a donkey - well he just stays still in the middle of the road, after all he has paid to use the road!

It is not just wild animals you need to watch out for on the roads. Further north you cross the veterinary line where the large farms stop and the communal lands start. Here the wildlife is much reduced but it is replaced by people, cattle and goats all whom tend to consider the road as some sort of magnet. Cattle seem to have no real regard for cars at all - if you see them slow down. If you see them heading towards the road slow down even more. At night they like to sit on the roads - or at least the black cows do! Again don't drive at night unless you have to.

Patterns of Diversity

In recent years a popular pastime for biologists is to map out where in the world or within a country you get the most species i.e. greatest biodiversity. This helps select priorities for conservation since most people think it best to first protect the places with the most species. The problem you face is that different groups of animals often turn out to have different diversity distributions. Take scorpions in Namibia. There are two areas with a high numbers of species. The first is between Windhoek and Swakopmund, the second is down south between Fish River Canyon and Keetmanshoop. Both areas have around 20 species. Contrast that with frog diversity which is greatest in the wet Caprivi. So which to conserve first? We probably figure that scorpions can survive fine without us but at present frogs are disappearing rather fast all over the world so maybe we should pick the Caprivi. This would fit with mammal conservation. The Caprivi being the hotspot with over 110 species of mammal compared to somewhere like Etosha that has more like the low eighties.

The bird diversity map would partly support this choice having the national hotspot at Mahango Game reserve which boats about 420 species. There are some pretty high centers of bird diversity in a line running from Etosha to Windhoek. The Waterberg Plateau Park sits in the middle of this line and is one of the peaks for bird diversity. These bird peaks match well with the plant diversity map. The plant diversity map throws a few extras of its own in. A series of smallish islands with high plant diversity go down the country. Many of these occur where there are changes of altitude and habitat.

One interesting features is the low diversity for all forms of life in the massive Namib Desert park. Not even scorpions are that diverse here.

Rather than diversity let's look at the number of endemic animals in a region. After all these are the animals that are either wholly, or to a large extent, only occurring in Namibia. When viewed from a global perspective there is a strong argument that these species should be the priorities for conservation work. Here the pattern is much more consistent. A large belt runs from the western Angolan border, down to Fish River Canyon. The band always stays a little bit inland from the coast. Rather ironically (for conservation) the band runs between Etosha and the Skeleton Coast parks, and down south runs outside most of the Namib Park.

The good news is when you look at where the large mammals occur. For large herbivores the main concentration both of species and number of species is a wide band starting around Etosha and heading down to Windhoek. The greatest concentrations seem to occur at the north east and south west corners of Etosha, along with an area to the north east of Windhoek. In places you can get up to 70 animals per square kilometer. For large carnivores the peak diversity is a strip running from the northern coast through Etosha and across to the border with Botswana. The main place where large carnivore and large herbivore diversity overlap is Etosha itself!

Further Reading

Birding in Namibia by Eckart Demasius & Christine Marais.
Published by Gamsberg Macmillan (Windhoek), 1999.
ISBN 99916-0-190-2
Covers 19 sites in Namibia giving checklists and a few details.
Nice pictures, plus a section on the birds endemic to Namibia.

Field Guide to Mammals of Southern Africa by Chris & Tilde
Stuart. Published by Struik (Cape Town), 2001.
ISBN 1 86872 537 5
Traditional style field guide with photographs for illustrations.
Has all the facts and figures, including distribution.

Atlas of Namibia by John Mendelsohn, Alice Jarvis, Carole
Roberts and Tony Robertson. Published by David Philip (Cape
Town). 2002.
ISBN 0-86486-516-3
A great fact filled book with maps on everything from wildlife
density to the mobile phone network.

A Photographic Guide to the Birds of Namibia by Ian and Jackie
Sinclair. Published by Struik (Cape Town). 1995.
ISBN 1 86825 730 4
Pocket size book with photographs and maps of the commoner
birds to be found in Namibia. Good when used in combination
with a more established guidebook

The Kingdom Field Guide to African Mammals by Jonathan
Kingdom. Published by Academic Press (San Diego). 1997.
ISBN 0-12-408355-2
A field guide with comprehensive and interesting descriptions of
the behavior and physiology of various African mammals.

The Safari Companion – A guide to Watching African Mammals by Richard Estes. Published by Chelsea Green Publishing Company (Vermont). 1993.
ISBN 0-930031-49-0
A guide to the behavior and social organisation of the larger African mammals

The Larger Illustrated Guide to Birds of Southern Africa by Ian Sinclair and Phil Hockey. Published by Struik (Cape Town). 1996.
ISBN 1 86825 759 2.
My favorite guide to the birds of Southern Africa – bit big to go in your pocket, and I wish they would produce a version with just the subset of species found in Namibia.

Notes on Nature by Amy Schoeman. Published by Gamsberg Macmillan (Windhoek). 2002.
ISBN 99916-0-326-3
A collection of nature notes that have been previously published elsewhere. Covers the big stuff, as well as insects, plants and landscape features.

A Field Guide to the Tracks and Signs of Southern and East African Wildlife by Chris and Tilde Stuart. Published by Struik (Cape Town). 2000.
ISBN 1 86872 558 8
A photographic guide covering lots of things to find in the bush like droppings, spoor, damage to vegetation, remains of food etc.

Assorted papers, articles and reports by Rob Simmons. This gentleman has published a lot of information relating to birds in Namibia. Use of the internet should help you track down most of the references.

Namibian Wildlife Society – hold monthly meetings and produces Roan News.

Namibian Bird Club – hold monthly meetings and produce a quarterly journal called Lanioturdus. They can be contacted at PO Box 67, Windhoek, Namibia.

Department of Environmental Affairs – http://www.dea.gov.na - These guys publish a fair deal of research about Namibian wildlife. Their website has lists of references along with data and reports.

www.ingramcontent.com/pod-product-compliance
Lightning Source LLC
Chambersburg PA
CBHW030413290526
45785CB00004B/1984